SoJourn

Volume 6, Number 1

A journal devoted to the history, culture, and geography of South Jersey

Summer 2021

SoJourn is a collaborative effort. Local historians contribute the articles; Stockton students—in this issue, the editing interns of spring 2021 and fall 2021—edit the articles, set the type, and design the layout; the directors of the South Jersey Culture & History Center at Stockton University oversee the publication. We are always seeking additional articles. If you have one, or more, contact us at the address or emails below.

Editors
The current team includes William Amend, Cynthia Anstey, Tyler Bolich, Kelsey Caban, Madison Chris, Amanda Clark, Katelyn Comer, Sierra Estremera, Gabriella Fiorica, Elizabeth Glass, Elena Gonzalez, Olivia Harris, Lea Hawthorne, Ethan Jardim, Maxwell Klenk, Salena LeDonne, Nyzira Lynn, Jay Marachese, Isabella Monacchio, Brianna Patterson, Jonathan Porro, Alison Roemer, Andrew Torres and James Wynne.

Supervising Editors
Tom Kinsella and Paul W. Schopp

ISSN: 2474-6665
ISBN: 978-1-947889-10-1
A publication of the South Jersey Culture & History Center
at Stockton University
www.stockton.edu/sjchc/

© 2021, the authors, South Jersey Culture & History Center, and Stockton University. All rights reserved.

Filler images, at the conclusion of articles, courtesy of the Paul W. Schopp Collection unless otherwise noted.

To contact SJCHC write:
SJCHC / School of Arts & Humanities
Stockton University
101 Vera King Farris Drive
Galloway, New Jersey
08205

Email:
Thomas.Kinsella@stockton.edu
Paul.Schopp@stockton.edu

About this Issue of *SoJourn*

An oft repeated axiom contains great truth: "the more you learn about South Jersey, the more you find out what you don't know." The eight counties comprising what we call South Jersey—Ocean, Burlington, Camden, Atlantic, Gloucester, Salem, Cumberland, and Cape May— provide a cultural and physical landscape unique and distinct from North Jersey. The social tapestry spread across South Jersey contains a diversity of experiences, ranging from the watermen who inhabit the coastal zones, to the skilled workers in glass and iron, to those seeking a utopian way of life, to the farmers that provided Abraham Browning with the moniker "the Garden State." The small, but growing, cities in South Jersey burgeoned with industrial enterprises, along with retail businesses to serve the factory employees. Shipyards dotted the numerous tributaries to the Delaware River, building wooden craft of all descriptions. As the railroads crisscrossed South Jersey, shipping and travel opportunities proliferated. The late nineteenth century witnessed the arrival of Jewish emigres in South Jersey, seeking to escape the horrors of the czarist pogroms, a type of ethnic holocaust. These Jews established agricultural colonies, along with small manufactures, during the 1880s and 1890s across Salem, Cumberland, Atlantic, and Cape May counties. We hope that this issue of *SoJourn*, like the preceding issues, will provide you with information unknown to you prior to reading the articles.

The contents of this issue offer a potpourri of topics. First-time contributor Gary Saretzky proffers "Careers in Camerawork: Six Photographers of Camden, New Jersey, 1860–1910," derived from his massive study of nineteenth-century New Jersey photographers. The editors selected "'Big Saturday' in the Pines" to reproduce in this issue. The Friday, August 1, 1845, edition of *The Burlington Gazette* yielded the original text, to which we added photographs, woodcuts, and engravings, along with reproducing details from the 1849 county map. Veteran author John Lawrence introduces us to the methodologies professional archaeologists employ in his article, "The Skinny on the Privy . . ." In collaboration with others, John conducted an investigation of the outdoor privy at the Red Dragon Canoe Club in Edgewater Park, Burlington County. Returning author and artist Hal Taylor has prepared a text and wonderful illustrations on the East Point Lighthouse and a visit by artist Andrew Wyeth. A republication of George Agnew Chamberlain's "Jarrad, Last of the Pineys," was originally found within the May 30, 1925, edition of *The Saturday Evening Post*. It still remains a timely article today. For his second *SoJourn* article, Dennis McDonald introduces the reader to super athlete George E. Weber, cyclist extraordinaire, who smashed many records before typhoid fever claimed his life at the young age of 20. Burlington resident Erik Burro recounts a story of a boy scout that risked his life to save his friends. Billy Bastian succumbed to his injuries a year after the serious accident that crushed his body, and mourners turned out in force for his funeral and interment. The serial publication of Joseph S. Reeves Jr.'s *Maurice River Memories* continues in this issue with two new installments. Dennis Niceler and friends prepared a memorial at the passing of Egg Harbor City historian Mark Maxwell. An article on the origins of Port Republic that I prepared rounds out the issue. Of course, we have included our usual filler material and advertisements for other publications.

Finally, a word about this issue's cover images. Riverine transportation of goods and people grew exponentially during the nineteenth century as innovation drove the development of larger and more powerful steamboats for use on the Delaware River, represented on this cover by the steamer BRISTOL (née SUE), the ADELAIDE, the MAJOR REYBOLD, the QUEEN ANNE, and, from the twentieth century, the STATE OF PENNSYLVANIA. Delaware River tributaries also generated traffic, albeit, the vessels were usually much smaller, often powered with steam, and often carried freight only. The DENNY BROTHERS represents this genre. The invention of the internal combustion engine provided a means to propel shallow-draft boats like the ALERT and the final form of the ANNABELL, operating on waterways of little depth. Specialty craft like the menhaden fishing boat NELLIE E. RAWSON and tugboats like WINFIELD S. CAHILL and the MINERVA fulfilled their individual purposes. The tugs often hauled sand barges and truck lighters. All these boats served to build the commerce and the economy up and down the Delaware River and its tributaries. As motorized highway vehicles became the preferred method of transportation, the commercial boat traffic quietly disappeared and the state soon began replacing formerly movable bridges with fixed spans to accommodate highway traffic.

We hope you enjoy this latest offering of *SoJourn*. Tom and I apologize for the issue's dilatory release, but both of us have been heavily involved in other projects that demanded our complete attention. We hope to return to a regular schedule with our next issue, which will be thematic for the Jersey Coast, including the Delaware Bay, River, and tributaries.

Paul W. Schopp

Assistant Director
South Jersey Culture & History Center
Stockton University

Map of Contents

KEY

- 🟡 "Careers in Camerawork: Six Photographers of Camden, New Jersey, 1860–1910" by Gary D. Saretzky, 7
- 🟢 "'Big Saturday' in the Pines: *The Burlington Gazette*, Friday, August 1, 1845" by Edmund Morris, 27
- 🔵 "The Skinny on the Privy: Investigation of the Shipman Mansion Privy" by John W. Lawrence, 33
- 🟠 "The Artist and the Lighthouse" by Hal Taylor, 47
- (Pine Barrens) "Jarrad, Last of the Pineys" by George Agnew Chamberlain, 51
- 🟤 "George E. Weber: Burlington County's Greatest Athlete" by Dennis McDonald, 61
- 🟢 "South Jersey Scout Hero" by Erik L. Burro, 69
- 🔵 "*Maurice River Memories*: 'Quackam's Beach' and 'Relatives'" by Joseph S. Reeves Jr., 75
- 🩷 "In Memoriam Mark Maxwell" by Dennis Niceler & Friends, 81
- 🟣 "The Sum of Its Parts: The Making of Port Republic" by Paul W. Schopp, 83

No Wild Rivers in South Jersey 46, *Growing American* 60, Call 98, list of *SoJourn* articles, 99.

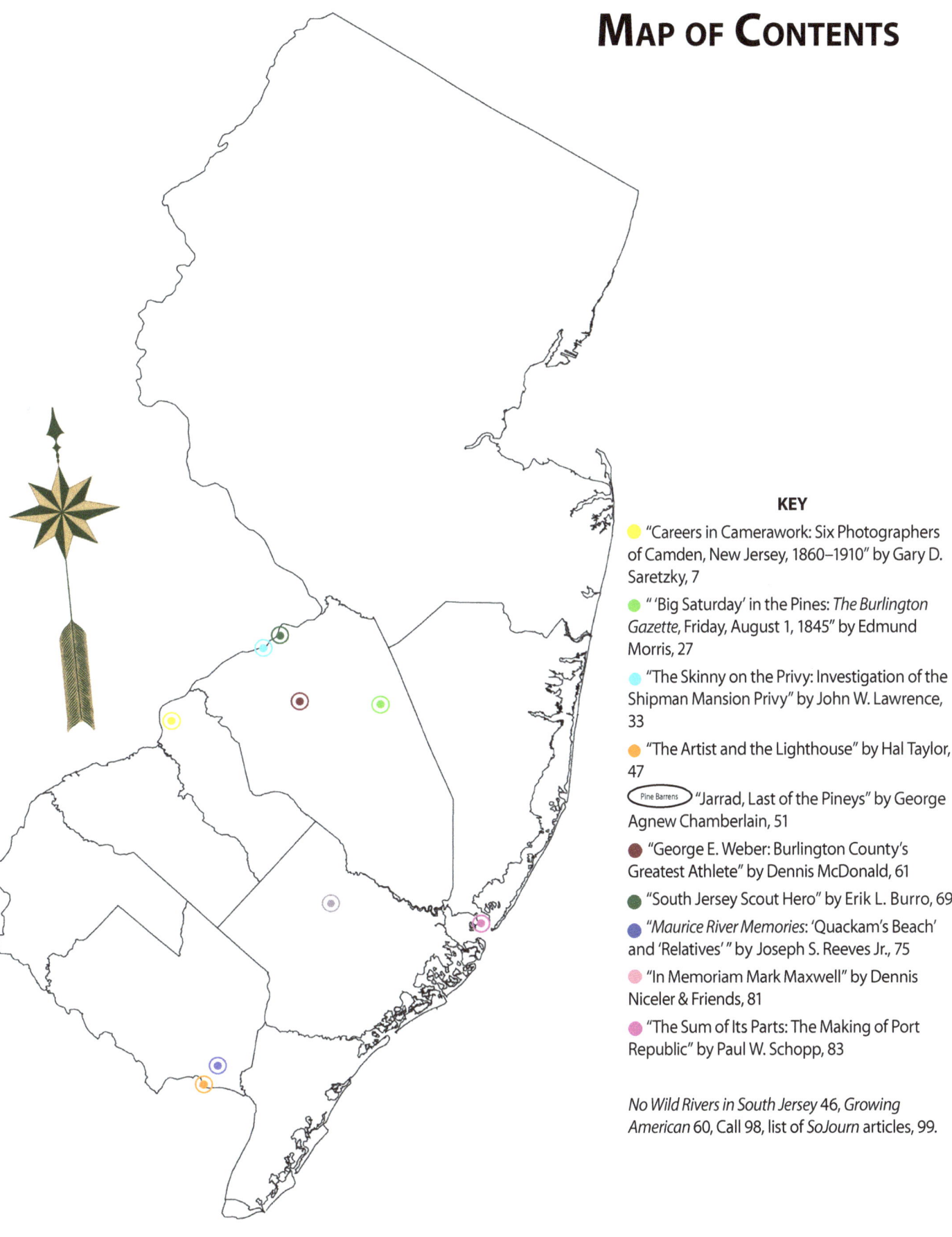

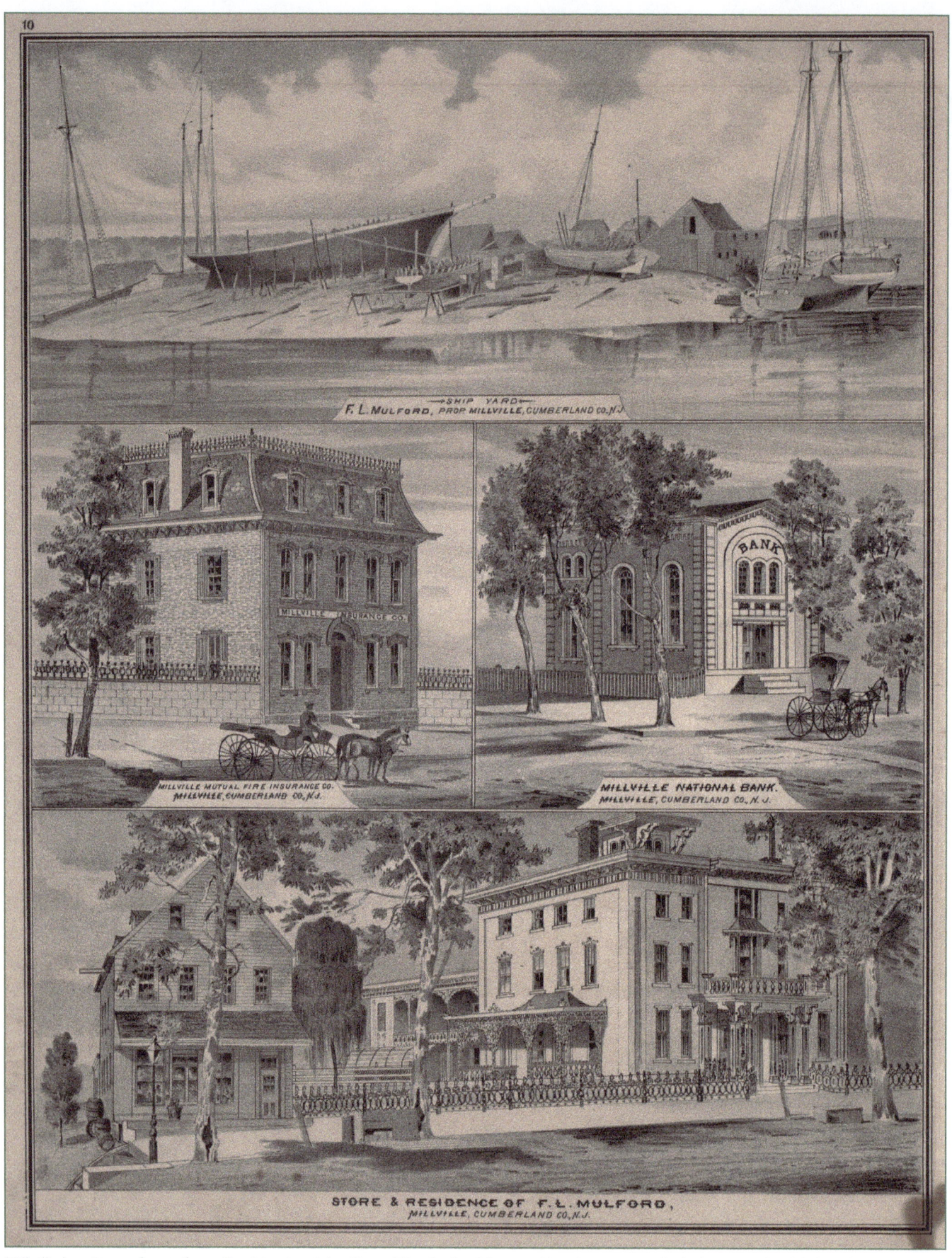

Millville locations of note from *Combination Atlas Map of Cumberland County, New Jersey*, compiled, drawn and published from personal examinations and surveys by D. J. Stewart (Philadelphia, 1876).

Careers in Camerawork:
Six Photographers of Camden, New Jersey, 1860–1910

Gary D. Saretzky

From the mid-nineteenth century until 1900, the history of photography in Camden, across the Delaware River from Philadelphia, parallels that of Jersey City and Hoboken in sight of New York City across the Hudson. From a small town of 3,371 residents in 1840, Camden grew to 75,935 by 1900, benefiting from its proximity to Philadelphia and transportation links in most directions by rail, road, and water.[1] The number of factories expanded, attracting immigrants and the surrounding rural population seeking employment. Soon, Camden became known for such industries as shipbuilding and, later in the century, Campbell Soup, incorporated in 1891. During the same period, the number of photographers also increased, some working in Camden and others, like their counterparts in Hudson County, becoming commuters to work across the river. Several Camden photographers had their own galleries in the bigger city during part of their careers, a not surprising development because of the increased commercial potential there, albeit with stiffer competition. A few maintained concurrent galleries on both sides of the river. While Camden photographers experienced considerable variation in their careers, for many of them, Philadelphia played a role.

Many who attempted to eke out a living with photography in the 1800s went on to other professions after a few years. Those artists included in this article had their own studios and remained photographers for a substantial period, but they are only a representative sample, and others did likewise in Camden. The six discussed in detail below provide an indication of the experiential range among Camden photographers who began their careers before 1900.

During the period 1850 to 1900, they were among about 300 professional photographers operating in the city of Camden, with about half the total owning their business for at least a short time.[2] Those located in census records and directories with home addresses may have only worked for photo gallery owners or other businesses in Camden but, more likely, commuted to work in Philadelphia.

As in many other towns, daguerreotypists who visited Camden in the 1850s often remained briefly and then moved on. Gabriel Moore, born in 1808, was the only daguerreotypist listed in the 1850 Camden directory. Others who followed him in that decade included John Hood and John C. Odling, the latter offering ambrotypes that began superseding daguerreotypes in the latter 1850s.

For all of New Jersey in the nineteenth century, there was approximately one photographer per 7,000 inhabitants, so it is not surprising to find only two photographers in the 1865 Camden city directory, when the population was about 17,000.[3] Andrews Sims, discussed below, was one of the two. The other was a deaf and dumb photographer and painter named Andrew B. Carlin (also found as Carter and Carten), who had a gallery in Camden from 1863 to 1868. In the 1870 Camden Census, the enumerator recorded him as 53, born in Pennsylvania, and working as an "artist painter" living with his wife Anna, 47, also deaf and dumb, and three children. Among other Camden photographers active in the 1860s, perhaps the most widely traveled was Lorenzo F. Fisler Jr., whose career began before Sims.

Lorenzo F. Fisler Jr.[4]

Born December 20, 1840, Fisler was the son of Dr. Lorenzo Fisler Sr., who served seven terms as mayor of Camden and wrote a history of the city.[5] By 1860, young Lorenzo was a photographer, probably working for his brother-in-law Walter Dinmore, who had married Lorenzo's older sister Abbie in 1859.[6] In partnership with Charles Warnick, Walter Dinmore had opened a photography business at 730 Chestnut in Philadelphia in 1858, but he relocated in 1863 to Shanghai, where he had a studio with his brothers Harry and Christopher.[7]

Early in the 1860s, according to a newspaper account published in 1891, Lorenzo met Japanese envoys in Philadelphia and accompanied them on their return. "Vicissitudes at sea" resulted in him arriving at a Chinese port and he spent most of the next 18 years in China, eventually marrying a young Chinese woman.[8]

Fisler's actual experience, however, probably differed from this article. The Japanese envoys visited Philadelphia in 1860. No reference to Fisler traveling abroad in 1860 has been found and Fisler only obtained a passport on July 8, 1861, a year after the Japanese had left, although the United States did not require passports for travel abroad at that time.[9] He probably remained home for two more years before departing. On June 5, 1863, he was a passenger aboard the medium clipper ship Talisman. Sailing through the South Atlantic off the coast of South America on its way to rounding Cape Horn, the Talisman soon encountered the highly successful Confederate raider Alabama. After forcing everyone off the sailing ship and robbing the vessel of its cargo and luggage, the belligerent crew burned the Talisman. Fisler and other passengers reached Rio de Janeiro, from where he returned home on August 11.[10]

Fisler then attempted a second trip to Shanghai, this time leaving from San Francisco on July 13, 1864. He arrived safely on September 14 and joined the Dinmores.[11] The Dinmores returned the United States after a few years and Fisler returned home for an extended visit from 1867 to early 1870. While traveling back to Shanghai, he stopped in Japan. Upon his return to China, he succeeded photographer Charles Weed on Canton Road, and offered such services as portraits, landscapes, and staged photographs.[12] His work included hand-colored cartes-de-visite of actors and courtesans, who probably used them for advertising and as souvenirs.[13] According to the 1891 article, he wintered in Shanghai and summered farther north in Tientsin (Tianjin), traveling extensively in China during his long sojourn there. Perhaps his most widely reproduced portrait, taken in Tianjin in 1875, was of Viceroy Li Hongzhang.[14] In one notable incident, he surreptitiously

Anonymous, Lorenzo F. Fisler, copy of a carte-de-visite, circa 1870, from an album once owned by Milton Miller (1830–1899), a photographer in China. Courtesy of Terry Bennett.

Lorenzo F. Fisler, Jr., Li Hung-Chang (Li Hongzhang), Viceroy of China, *Far East*, September 1876. Courtesy of Terry Bennett.

Lorenzo F. Fisler, Jr., Sir Thomas Francis Wade, British Minister to China, *Far East*, August 1876. Courtesy of Terry Bennett.

entered the Forbidden City with a photographer friend and took what he claimed were the first two photos of the "Palace of the Earth's Repose, Harem of the Emperor of China," which he said contained 150 concubines ruled by the Empress and attended by more than 500 slaves.[15]

In the early 1870s, Fisler became seriously ill and an English-speaking Methodist Chinese teenager named Alena nursed him back to health. He then married her in 1872 when she was about 15 years old.[16] Fisler's family expressed displeasure that he married a Chinese woman, but in 1884 he returned with her to Camden.[17] He soon established a photo business described as "Landscape & Mechanical Photographers" in partnership with Theodore F. Gaubert. The partnership lasted until 1887.[18] Sometime in the mid-1880s, he reportedly made two tintypes of Walt Whitman with his young friend, Bill Duckett.[19]

Fisler continued to be listed as a photographer in Camden into the early 1900s, but examples of photographs from this phase of his career have not been found by this author. In 1891, he took over the gallery of the recently deceased E. J. Hunt at 321 Federal Street and announced that he would destroy Hunt's negatives in two months.[20] Short-lived, this gallery failed to be listed in the 1892 Camden directory. The 1898 directory lists Fisler as a photographer living in Camden and working in Philadelphia and it is quite possible that he had obtained employment in the city during other years. In 1910, he offered numerous negatives taken in China and Japan for sale; whether any purchaser came forward or any of these negatives exist today has not been determined.[21] Fisler continued being listed in Camden directories as a photographer through 1912, but only with residential, not business, addresses. He died on November 18, 1918, and was buried at South Laurel Hill Cemetery in Philadelphia where his parents lie in repose.[22] Laurel Hill told Fisler's wife that because she was Chinese, she could not be buried there when she died, so in 1923 she had Lorenzo moved to Evergreen Cemetery in Camden, where she joined him in 1929.[23]

Andrew Sims

Born in 1830 in Scotland, Andrew Sims purchased a one-way ticket to the United States in 1858 and settled initially at 811 Federal Street, Camden, with his wife Mary and children. Tragedy struck when their youngest child, Andrew Jr., died in 1860 at the age of four. By 1900, only six of their eleven children had survived, a high proportion but not unusual at that time.

Andrew Sims seems to have led a blameless life, as the few mentions of him in newspapers do not pertain to anything negative. He began his career in Camden, if not previously in Scotland, as a gilder, and listed the profession "picture framer" when he registered for the military draft in 1863.[24] By 1865, he had established a photography gallery at 232 Federal Street, where he also sold looking glasses (mirrors) and picture frames, no doubt gilded by the proprietor.[25] He became active in the Third Street Methodist Episcopal Church and eventually became a trustee and a religious classroom teacher.[26] By 1870, he joined the YMCA Board of Managers. Sims' apparently sober social life included membership in the Sparkling Water Division, No. 163, of the Sons of Temperance.

Sims, who moved his business to 215 Federal Street in 1868, created a substantial number of cartes-de-visite (cdv) portraits in the 1860s and 1870s, each with a notice on the back, "Special attention to copying ambrotypes and other pictures into large or small photographs." One cdv portrait taken in the 1860s was of Chaplain John H. Frazee of the 3rd New Jersey Cavalry, a copy of which is at the New Jersey State Archives. His photographs of children included post-mortems, a common practice in the days of high infant mortality. In 1874, he relocated to 307 Market Street, where he

Andrew Sims, girl with picture book on fringed posing chair, carte-de-visite, late 1860s. Author's digital collection.

Andrew Sims, standing boy holding a hat with elbow on table, carte-de-visite, late 1860s. Author's digital collection.

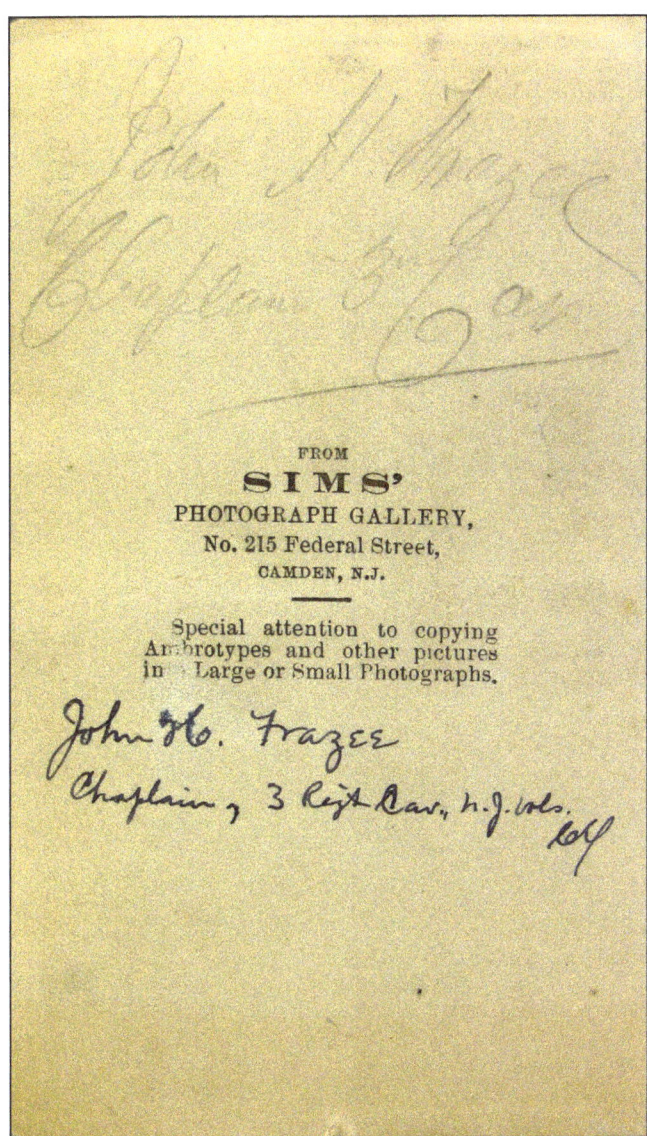

Andrew Sims, Chaplain John H. Frazee, 3rd New Jersey Cavalry, carte-de-visite, recto and verso, late 1860s. New Jersey State Archives.

remained until 1885. His ad placed in 1875 offered four tintypes ("ferreotypes") for twenty-five cents and in 1878, he offered large framed photographs for $1.50, the equivalent of about $30 today.[27] In 1879, he opened a branch gallery at 202 S. 2nd Street in Philadelphia that lasted about a year. That building, a few blocks from where the ferry from Camden stopped at Vine Street,[28] housed a series of photographers from 1865 to 1885.

The 1880 Census of Products of Industry for Camden provides insights into Sims' work at that time. He had invested $2,500 in his business and had two male employees whom he paid $2.50 per day for skilled labor and $.82 per day for unskilled. For the previous year ending June 1, 1880, he had paid $1,040 in wages. During this period, his cost of materials was $320 and the value of his products, $2,180. His workday was 10 hours, and he was open 12 months a year.

Clearly, Sims was not becoming wealthy and there are some indications that his photography business declined in the 1870s. Examples of his work after the early 1870s are much less commonly found today than his earlier portraits and in 1879, Sims made space in his Camden showroom for a jeweler, Charles E. Smith, suggesting that he needed to increase his income.[29] Sims' finances may have improved after his son Leonard, born in 1863, began working for his father as a photographer in 1882 at a new gallery, Sims and Son, at 737 Race Street, Philadelphia. With the addition of son John, who died at age 29 in 1890, it became Sims and Sons, and continued in business until 1896 with at least two relocations.[30]

watchman.³¹ The 1910 Census found Andrew and his wife Mary of sixty years at 811 Raymond Avenue living with Leonard and Leonard's second wife Virginia; Leonard had become a bank messenger. Andrew Sims was listed as an alien, so it is likely that he never underwent naturalization to become an American citizen. Mary died December 10, 1915, and Andrew followed her on November 18, 1917, at the age of 90. They were buried in Harleigh Cemetery.³²

Frederick H. and William R. Fearn³³

Compared to Sims, the Fearn family history was punctuated by more dramatic events. Frederick H. Fearn and William R. Fearn were sons of John Fearn and Amelia Ann Hearn, who married on February 2, 1846, at St. Leonard's Church in the Shoreditch district in the East End of London, England.³⁴ The Fearns emigrated to New York in 1850 with their infant son John, and initially lived in Brooklyn, where the 1850 federal decennial Census enumerated father John as a dyer.³⁵ He then found work as a hat presser for at least fifteen years. After Frederick was born in Queens about 1853, the Fearns settled in Staten Island, where William was born in 1858.³⁶

Inflating his age, Frederick joined the U.S. Navy when he was about 15. On January 29, 1868, he shipped out of New York on the U.S.S. Franklin as a landsman, the lowest rank, and as such would have performed unskilled labor. In September 1871, he contracted gonorrhea while the Franklin was in Nice, France, and by November, he occupied a bed in the U.S. Naval Hospital in Chelsea, Massachusetts. The doctor transferring him to the hospital wrote that his case "has lately become unusually troublesome" and that Fearn also suffered from phimosis, not altogether uncommon among uncircumcised men.³⁷

By the 1870 Census, while Frederick served in the Navy, his father John had become a photographer in Middletown, a municipality in Staten Island incorporated in 1860 from parts of Southfield and Castleton.³⁸ No doubt, his father instilled an interest in photography in William, who was twelve in 1870. But John did not remain a photographer. By 1875, John and Amelia relocated to Camden, New Jersey, where they lived at 433 Market Street for about seven years. John had become a "medical electrician," a term used by those who sought to use "galvanism" to rejuvenate or cure patients with an electrical current from a galvanic battery.³⁹ Amelia also practiced galvanism at their residence and advertised her services.⁴⁰

Andrew Sims, "Will" (young man with bow tie), ferrotype card, recto and verso, 1870s. Author's collection.

Meanwhile, Sims kept the Camden location open until 1885 and continued living nearby. He was listed as a photographer with home address only in city directories until 1904 and thereafter was identified as a

Fern's [Fearn's], Camden, George M. Rainear, cabinet card, circa 1890. Author's collection.

A death disrupted the Fearns' electrical medicine practice in 1881. In April, Robert Moore, 22, died after treatment by "Dr. Fearn" for pneumonia. Mr. Fearn filed the death certificate, stating that Moore had expired from bronchial consumption and signed it, "John Fearn, M.E." (Medical Electrician). The coroner inquired at the County Clerk's office and learned that Fearn had not registered his medical diploma as required by law. Fearn immediately left Camden after posting a sign on his premises stating that he had "removed to Broad street, fourth door above York street, Philadelphia."[41] John Fearn is not mentioned again as a medical practitioner in the Camden newspapers but the Fearns apparently returned to the town. Amelia began advertising again in the *Courier-Post* (Camden) in 1883, with an address of 627 Clinton Street.[42]

John and Amelia again appeared on the pages of the *Morning Post* in 1884, when they sued the West Jersey Ferry Company over a sprained wrist Amelia suffered. *The Philadelphia Inquirer* provided the added information that she had slipped on ice and snow that crew members had failed to remove from the ferry deck while in the slip at the Market Street ferry house in Philadelphia.[43] The suit proved unsuccessful, but Amelia persisted. In 1891, the Supreme Court of Pennsylvania heard her appeal of the case she had lost in Common Pleas court. Her attorneys argued that although she had previously sued only for her injury, her husband also fell, landing on a cleat while carrying a heavy galvanic battery, and that he succumbed from his injuries in 1888. The Court ruled that the ferry company could not be held responsible because it could not reasonably be expected to keep the snow off the deck during a storm.[44]

While John and Amelia were involved in quasi-medical work, Frederick and William became photographers in Camden. Frederick was a photographer by 1878 when the *Morning Post* reported that he was arrested by officer Randall at Federal Street, next to the Post Office, for

> an alleged indignity perpetrated upon Delia Hann, a girl nine years of age, living with her mother at 303 Federal street. The details are too revolting to make public, the little girl having been induced, after sitting for her picture, to go into a dark rear room, where she was subject to insult and outrage without knowing the nature of the offense owing to the darkness. Mayor Ayers will investigate.

The following day, the *Morning Post* published an update that Mrs. Hann, the mother of the little girl, as well as Fearn, stated that "the whole affair as given by Officer Randall, is wrong, and that her little girl made no such statement as represented."[45] So the case was dropped.

The younger brother, William Fearn, began his working career as an upholsterer[46] but by 1879 the brothers had formed a photography partnership, when the *Morning Post* reported that Frederick and William Fearn had a photographic wagon on the corner of 5th & Market. They had a dispute about business matters and Frederick, in company with a man named Lewis Kupp, smashed the wagon to pieces. Frederick and Kupp were arrested, charged with malicious mischief, and held on $100 bail each.[47] William left town, possibly a result of this fraternal strife. By 1880, he was working as a photographer for, and living with, the highly respectable cameraman, Theodore M. Schleier in Nashville, Tennessee.[48] He returned to Camden by 1882.[49] Apparently, the brothers reached a rapprochement, for in 1883, they began to be listed as Fearn Brothers at 326 Federal Street. However, it appears that often they did not operate there simultaneously, and "Brothers" was soon dropped from the name. William ran it for a year, then turned it over to Frederick, who operated it until 1890. Frederick then moved to Trenton where he opened a new gallery and William returned to run the operation in Camden until September 1893, when J. E. Smith succeeded him, probably the John E. Smith, photographer, who had a gallery in Bordentown from 1869 to 1897.[50]

The Fearns' 326 Federal Street studio was on the second floor and by 1890, employed four assistants. To attract patrons, the gallery ran ads in the *Courier-Post*. In 1885, it offered Bon Tons (tintypes) for 50 cents per dozen and cabinet cards for $1.50 per dozen.[51] While the brothers took turns operating the gallery in Camden, they were active elsewhere in the area as photographers. In 1882 and 1883, Frederick worked as photographer in Philadelphia while living in Camden but did not have his own studio. In 1887, William had a gallery in Haddonfield, Camden County. From January to March of that year, the *Courier-Post* ran his ad, "Go to W. R. Fearn, for Fine Cabinet Photographs at Haddonfield, Main Street, near Braddock's Drug Store. N.B. This is not F. H. Fearn of Camden. I have no connection with any other gallery."[52] William then operated in Philadelphia at 120 S. 2nd Street in 1888 and 1889 before returning to Camden upon Frederick's departure.

Fearn's (probably Frederick Fearn), Camden, woman with umbrella, cabinet card, 1880s. Author's collection.

After turning over the Camden gallery to J. E. Smith in 1893, William continued to be listed as a photographer in the city directories until 1898, when the directory described him as a salesman. In 1899, he returned to his youthful occupation of upholsterer and continued in that trade until around 1910, when the 1910 federal decennial Census listed him as a carpenter. He subsequently became a building contractor in Camden until 1923, when he and his wife Anna moved to Glendale, California, where they joined their married daughter Lucy and her husband William Ziegler, a printer who worked as a compositor for newspapers.[53] William and Anna had married in 1877 and had four children, two of whom survived to 1900, including Lucy.[54] The couple seem to have had a stable family life, except for the early deaths of two children.

By comparison, Frederick's home life was turbulent. After his discharge from the Navy, he came to Camden and married Annie Lawrence. By 1880, they had three children: Walter, 6; Louis, 4; and George, 11 months.[55] At the age of 26, Annie died of consumption on December 6, 1883, less than two months after giving birth to a daughter, Pansey, delivered by her grandmother Amelia who served as midwife.[56] Frederick soon found another spouse. On July 2, 1884, he married sixteen-year-old Georgianna Reed of Camden.[57] A month later, their daughter Bertha was born.[58]

Frederick Fearn and Georgianna made headlines in October 1886. Newspapers reported demonstrations and court actions against them for sending Frederick's sons Walter, Louis, and George to reform school in Jamesburg, New Jersey, as incorrigibles. Although Fearn denied it, when he married his second wife, he allegedly agreed to get rid of the children from the first marriage and the couple neglected the children, forcing them to eat out of garbage cans. A mob of boys estimated at 2000–3000 burned an effigy of Fearn in front of his home. The mob carried banners and lighted Chinese lanterns, demanding that Fearn leave town. On another night, a brass band passed his house, followed by a parade of demonstrators, but the city police force prevented them from stopping at the house. A court-appointed attorney representing the children found two dozen witnesses who said the boys were docile.

Fearn's mother Amelia took a leading role in petitioning the court to get the boys returned. The youngest child was sent home because he was seven and the minimum age at the Jamesburg reform school was eight. The two older boys came back on October 27 by order of Judge Parker, who said that if the stepmother continued to abuse them, the neighbors should have her arrested, but he condemned the rioting. Fearn testified that if the children were returned, he would have to separate from his wife. The judge said he would try to find another home for the boys, and it is likely that their grandmother Amelia took custody, at least temporarily.[59] With her stepsons out of the way, Georgianna had four more children of her own by 1895.[60]

Frederick Fearn opened a new gallery at 23 S. Broad Street in Trenton by the spring of 1890. He called his business, Excelsior Photo Co., instead of using his surname.[61] On April 12, 1890, he made front page news again with his arrest for assault and battery on his wife and held for $300 bail.[62]

Frederick's mother Amelia also appeared in Trenton in 1890.[63] In March and April 1891, she advertised as Dr. A. Fearn, Medical Electrician, at 240 E. State Street,

Excelsior Photo Co. (Frederick Fearn), Trenton, boy in Fauntleroy costume, circa 1894, cabinet card. Author's collection.

promising to treat "all chronic and female disease. No shocks given.... The poor treated free each Tuesday."[64] She may also have helped in providing care for her grandchildren.

Fearn seems to have been sufficiently well behaved in the 1890s to keep his name out of the newspapers. Beginning in 1895, Excelsior advertised regularly in the *Trenton Evening Times*. That year, he offered 16 x 20 portraits enlarged from tintypes and daguerreotypes, for $3.00.[65] In 1897, he moved the gallery to 306 E. State, succeeding John H. Britton, where he competed with, among others, Edward S. Dunshee at 209 E. State Street.[66] In 1899, he offered cabinet cards for 75 cents per dozen (a very low price), 16 x 20 crayon portraits with six cabinet cards for $2.50 with a free frame, and 10 little Penny Photos for 10 cents.[67]

The Frederick Fearn family had some near tragedies but also an addition in the early 1900s. In December 1900, Frederick and Georgianna's 13-year-old son Clifford fell through the ice and went under. Fortunately, he was rescued and returned home to his mother, who had heard he had drowned.[68] In January 1901, Georgianna had another baby girl named Etta[69] and that year she took all six children to Atlantic City for the summer.[70] In 1903, two of the girls were hospitalized with typhoid fever but they recovered.[71]

On March 14, 1904, Frederick Fearn died in Trenton after a few years of failing health. Members of the Sons of Union Veterans served as pallbearers and he was buried in Greenwood Cemetery.[72] Georgianna immediately applied for a Civil War widow's pension on March 24.[73] She married James W. Hickey in 1905 and, after some time in Philadelphia, where she had a son, Arthur Frank, on August 4, 1910, the Hickeys moved to Atlantic City.[74] Georgianna outlived Frederick by more than 50 years. She died on March 22, 1956, at the age of 88.[75]

Edward F. Sherman and Mary C. Sherman

The story of Edward Franklin Sherman and his wife Mary ends sadly. Their tragedy involved events of national significance that should be remembered with abhorrence more than a century after Edward's untimely death.

Edward F. Sherman was born in Pottsville, Schuylkill County, Pennsylvania, on June 22, 1857, to Josiah and Malvina Sherman, both born in Maine. Josiah was a schoolteacher in Pottsville, but by 1870, he had become a professor at the Pennsylvania Female College (PFC) in Trappe, Montgomery County. PFC, legislatively chartered in 1853, educated about 1000 young women before it closed in 1880 and was located just down the street from Ursinus College, then limited to men. Edward, as "Frank Sherman," attended Ursinus in 1871–1872.[76]

After his service on the PFC faculty, Josiah Sherman found work as a teacher in Elwood, Atlantic County, New Jersey, near the Jersey Shore. The 1880 federal decennial Census, enumerated Josiah there with his wife and son Josiah (Jr.), a 20-year-old store clerk. Edward's whereabouts in 1880 has not been determined but on April 28, 1883, he married Mary Carol Platte in Camden. Born in Pennsylvania in June 1866, Mary's parents were Anne E. and William Platte, a paper mill worker. In 1880, they lived in Bass River in Burlington County, New Jersey. At the time of their marriage, Edward was residing in Elwood and Mary in Harrisville, which is now a paper mill ghost town in the Pine Barrens not far from Bass River.

Records for Edward and Mary Sherman after their marriage are unfortunately obscure until 1897, when the Camden directory listed Edward's Crystal Type Photograph Co., which lasted a year. On November 17, 1898, the *Courier-Post* (Camden) announced, "Camden's Newest Photographer. Sherman, the artist-photographer, has opened a ground floor studio, corner Broadway and Washington. His reliable agents will canvass the city and give especial low prices to introduce his beautiful photographs."[77] Mary, who remained childless, undoubtedly was involved in the business, as later evidence shows. By December 1901, they apparently needed help and advertised in *The Philadelphia Inquirer*, "Photo Finisher. The highest salary and traveling car fare will be paid [a] young lady who can trim, mount and spot platinum prints."[78] In the early 1900s, most photographers provided their customers with gelatin silver prints, not platinum, which while very high quality with a fine gradation of tones and greater permanency than gelatin, was more expensive to produce.[79] The Shermans' use of platinum suggests that their clientele included the affluent.

Like other local businessmen who found it both beneficial and pleasurable to join a fraternal order, Edward Sherman became a member of the King David Lodge of the Odd Fellows. On July 3, 1902, an article in the *Courier Post* noted, "There are brethren who are worthy of elevation to the highest honors which the lodge can confer, notably Brother E. F. Sherman, the photographer, who has rendered unusual services and demonstrated great executive ability." It appears that Sherman was a well-respected, law abiding, photographer who was doing well in Camden.[80]

Edward F. or Mary C. Sherman. Armory, in *Camden, New Jersey: The City's Rise and Growth* (1904). From copy at Camden County Historical Society.

In August 1902, local newspapers featured Edward Sherman with his portrait and text of his lengthy oration at the reunion of the Scottish-Irish branch of the Sherman family in Cape Cod Point, near Bar Harbor, Maine. Sherman apparently took a deep interest in his genealogy. He stated that his family descended from a William Sherman, who emigrated from England to Salem, Massachusetts, in 1629, where his widow and daughter married into the family of Myles Standish, the military officer who helped administer the Plymouth Colony. But he also traced the Shermans farther back to barbarians from Central Asia who in 450 A.D. landed in Britain and he digressed at length to recount the history of the Pilgrims and other tangential topics. The *Camden-Post Telegram* generously allocated almost an entire page of the newspaper to Sherman's speech.[81]

Sherman did so well in the photo business that on June 25, 1904, he announced the opening of a new South Studio on Broadway near Walnut and that Mary would oversee the current studio at Broadway and Washington (427 Broadway), which henceforth would be known as Sherman's North Studio. He stated that he would operate the South Studio (934 Broadway) but by appointment would "make sittings at the North Studio for platinum photographs." He continued, "The long and successful practice that Mrs. Sherman has had under the [electric] light makes it necessary that she should have the exclusive use of a light, as nearly as possible, to accommodate her growing patronage....." Sherman claimed to have introduced the electric lamp to photography studios in Camden. He assured readers that they were ready and willing to photograph customers at night, although he preferred them to visit during the day. He also declared that the Shermans now would be open by appointment on Sundays so they would no longer lose business to their competitors. At the South Studio, he planned to specialize in low-priced photographs, large portraits copied from small ones, sittings at night, and large group portraits.[82]

In the same year they opened the second gallery, the Shermans took time to go on separate trips. In August 1904, Edward went to Maine and Boston, where he attended the convention of New England photographers. When he returned on August 29, Mary and her assistant, Miss Josephine P. Gomez, left for a ten-day vacation to New York, New Haven, and other places in Connecticut.[83] These travels suggest that the Shermans were enjoying their prosperity.

Although the Shermans specialized in portraits, they also performed outdoor work and published lithographed postcards featuring their views of Camden. In 1904, the Camden Board of Trade published a promotional book, *Camden, New Jersey*, profusely illustrated with half-tone illustrations by the Sherman firm, including depictions of, among others, the Armory, City Hall, Cooper Hospital, and the Masonic building, as well as streetscapes. The book also featured an advertisement with an appealing photo credited to Mary C. Sherman of a little girl and boy, the latter holding a chicken. The advertisement boldly proclaims Sherman's North Studio with the address and "Mary C. Sherman, Artist," and below that, "Mr. Sherman makes sittings at the North Studio by appointment only. Platinum Prints in Sepia and Black." The South Studio is listed in a smaller font below. The prominence given to Mary Sherman in this advertisement over her husband is striking and implies the significance of her contribution to the success of the couple's business.[84]

The Shermans continued the North Studio from 1905 to 1907 and then consolidated their efforts at the South Studio at 934 Broadway, where they also lived. Edward likely retired in 1912, when the Camden directory listed him only with a home address and Mary

Edward F. and Mary C. Sherman, advertisement for Sherman studios in Camden with photography by Mary C. Sherman, *Camden, New Jersey: The City's Rise and Growth* (1904). From copy at the Camden County Historical Society.

was listed in the business directory. In 1913, neither was listed, as they had decided to winter in Florida and come back to New Jersey in the summers. For two winters beginning in 1912, they wintered in St. Petersburg, where they conducted a photo studio, and summered in Wildwood, New Jersey, the site of their seasonal gallery.[85] The Shermans soon purchased and moved to a bungalow on a property in a rural area outside St. Petersburg where they had eleven African American farm workers clearing the land and doing other jobs that Sherman hoped would help with subdivision and sale.

The couple's plans for a pleasant retirement terminated violently when Edward Sherman was brutally murdered at his winter home on November 11, 1914. During the night, a man fired a shotgun at his head while he lay sleeping in his bed near an open window. Mary was robbed, dragged out of the house, assaulted, and severely beaten. Reviving, she saw that her husband was dead and lost consciousness again for several hours. Awakening at 3 a.m., she managed to get help from the nearest neighbor about a half mile distance. She said that two African American men had committed the crime but could not identify them. Gangs of white vigilantes terrorized the Black community searching for suspects and hundreds of innocent African American residents fled by boat and foot. One who did not run away was John Evans, who had recently been let go by Sherman. Despite flimsy evidence, the vigilantes tortured Evans while he consistently maintained his innocence. After he was taken to jail, a mob of 1,500 white men and women forcibly removed him from incarceration and lynched him. Ebenezer Tobin, another Sherman employee, was arrested and tried on September 17, 1915. Mary Sherman returned for the trial from Camden, where she was still recuperating from a fractured skull, and testified that she recognized Tobin's voice, although she could not identify either of the men by sight. Tobin was convicted after the jury deliberated for fifteen minutes; he was executed on October 22.[86]

Mary left Florida and did not reopen a photography gallery in Camden, although she may have retained

Edward F. or Mary C. Sherman, Camden and Burlington, N.J. White-haired bearded man, cabinet card, early 1900s. Author's collection.

a financial interest in the Wildwood location. The 1915 New Jersey State Census for Camden records Mary as a 48-year-old photographer living with a couple about her age. In the 1920 federal decennial Census, the enumerator listed her as a widow without a profession residing with a family in Haddonfield near Camden.[87]

Concluding Remarks

Nineteenth- and early twentieth-century photographers in Camden faced the same challenges as their colleagues elsewhere, including competition, health issues, criminality, and deaths of spouses and children. Although their photographic products were broadly similar, each photographer had unique backgrounds, experiences, and personalities that shaped their lives and helped determine their degree of financial success. Some like Lorenzo F. Fisler were adventurous; others stayed close to home with gallery moves and branch studios commonplace in an effort to expand business. Photographers like Fisler and Edward F. Sherman, whose fathers were a doctor and a college teacher respectively, had good educations and began with advantages over those with less schooling. Regardless of how they started out in life, however, those like Andrew Sims demonstrated that dedication, diligence, and earning a good reputation could lead to financial stability, while the lives of the Fearn brothers show that even within one family, there can be significant variance. Mary C. Sherman's career serves to remind us that the number of women in photography increased substantially in the 1890s and early 1900s. While women photographers remained in the minority, their work appeared regularly in photographic journals and exhibits.[88]

About the Author

Gary D. Saretzky, archivist, educator, and photographer, worked as an archivist for more than fifty years at the State Historical Society of Wisconsin, Educational Testing Service, and the Monmouth County Archives. Saretzky taught the history of photography at Mercer County Community College, 1977–2012, and served as coordinator of the Public History Internship Program for the Rutgers University History Department, 1994–2016. He has published more than 100 articles and reviews on the history of photography, photographic conservation, and other topics, including "Nineteenth-Century New Jersey Photographers," in the journal, *New Jersey History*, Fall/Winter 2004, a revised version of which is available at http://saretzky.com.

Endnotes

1 Rail service from Camden to New York began early in 1835 and the first railroad bridge across the Delaware to Philadelphia was completed in 1896. Ferries operated across the Delaware River between Philadelphia and Camden and river steamers made regular trips up and down the river.
2 Author's database on Nineteenth-Century New Jersey Photographers, abstracted at http://saretzky.com.
3 The population figure of 17,000 is about the median between the 1860 and 1870 censuses, respectively 14,358 and 20,045. By 1900, there were at least ten studios, plus a firm that did printing. Quantitative data on photographers from author's database, op. cit. The estimate of 300 does not include about 50 photographers found outside Camden in Camden County.
4 This essay on Fisler was significantly enhanced with help from Bette Epstein, New Jersey State Archives, and Terry Bennett, author of the authoritative, well-illustrated volume, *History of Photography in China: Western Photographers, 1861–1879* (London: Quaritch), 2010. Karen Penn, a descendant of Fisler's great uncle Joseph Fisler, and Suzanne Schwartzwalder also assisted my research.
5 Birth of Lorenzo Jr. from death certificate, New Jersey State Archives. Re Lorenzo Fisler Sr. (1797–1871), see George R. Prowell, *The History of Camden County, New Jersey* (Philadelphia: L. J. Richards & Co., 1886), 270, 332, 430–31; Prowell mentions Lorenzo Sr.'s history of Camden published as a pamphlet in 1858 (copy at Camden County Historical Society). See also *Transactions of the Medical Society of New Jersey, 1871* (Newark: Jennings & Hardman), 173–74, 246–47; and "The Mortuary Roll: Deceased Physicians of Camden County," *Morning Post* (Camden), February 15, 1887. Lorenzo Jr. was the fourth child of Lorenzo Sr. and Anna Maria (Risley) Fisler (1818–1891). His younger brother Weston "Wes" Fisler (1843–1922) became a well-known professional baseball player in Philadelphia. Lorenzo Jr. also played baseball but not professionally.
6 The Fisler family was recorded twice in the 1860 federal decennial Census of Philadelphia. On July 14, the census schedule records Lorenzo (indexed in Ancestry.com as Lovenga Filer, born in England) as a photographist (photographer who made photographs on paper, as contrasted with daguerreotypists, ambrotypists, and ferreotypists), and his brother Richard as a clerk. In the other census record (indexed as Fester), recorded on July 11, the professions of the brothers are reversed. It is very likely that Lorenzo was the photographist in 1860 as there is no other indication that Richard ever worked in photography. In any case, Lorenzo was a photographist by June 1863, when he gave that profession in his registration for the military draft. U.S. Civil War Draft Registrations Records, 1863–1865. Ancestry.com.
7 Walter arrived in Shanghai on September 8, 1863. Initially, the brothers worked in the studio of J. Newman, who departed in 1864. Bennett, 110, 416.
8 "The Chinese Rebellion: An Interesting Chat with Lorenzo Fisler," *Morning Post* (Camden), December 8, 1891, 1. The Japanese envoys left on June 30, 1860.
9 U.S. Passport Applications, 1795–1925. Fisler obtained another passport on March 19, 1863.
10 After his return, reported in *West Jersey Press*, August 19, 1863, Fisler wrote "My First Voyage," *West Jersey*

Press, August 26, 1863, and continued September 2. In 1875, Fisler received $1,722.80 compensation for his lost photographic equipment, paid by the British government. "Alabama Claims," *Boston Post*, October 22, 1875, 2. Reported as about $2,500 in "'Lorry' Fisler and the Alabama Claims," *West Jersey Press*, November 17, 1875. For a judgment summary, see *Congressional Serial Set*, (Washington, DC: Government Printing Office), 1895, 4289–90.

11 Rev. J. M. W. Farnham, D.D., of Shanghai recalled, "Dinmore Bros. and L. F. Fisler, now of Philadelphia, and C. L. Weed, were among the first photographers that I can remember in Shanghai." "Dry Plates in a Damp Climate," *International Annual of Anthony's Photographic Bulletin*, 1891, vol. 3, 375–77, but Terry Bennett, op. cit., discusses several Chinese and foreign predecessors dating back to the early 1850s.

12 Bennett, 116. Walter Dinmore relocated from Shanghai to Baltimore and was a photographer there from 1866 to 1875, when he began working for about a year in Philadelphia as chief photographer at W. D. Clayton's Gallery of Photography with a residence in Camden. While there, he made a portrait of Walt Whitman. In 1885–1886, he had his own gallery in Philadelphia. Walter died May 13, 1895, of "apoplexy." Evergreen Cemetery Plot Burials, Reel 2, 38, Camden County Historical Society. Harrison "Harry" Dinmore had a gallery in Manayunk near Philadelphia, from 1889 to 1892. He later moved to New Jersey, where he had galleries in Palmyra (1910) and Absecon (1915) before his death on March 10, 1918. *The Philadelphia Inquirer*, March 12, 1918, 17.

13 Patented by A. A. E. Disderi in 1854 in France, the carte-de-visite was a small photograph mounted on a card approximately 2 3/8 x 4 inches, usually with the photographer's imprint on the back.

14 Roberta Wue, "The Mandarin at Home and Abroad: Picturing Li-Hongzhang," *Ars Orientalis* 43 (2013), 140–56, esp. 145; Bennett, 113–23.

15 This story, based on an interview by Alba Satterthwaite, was published in several newspapers, including "Adventure in China," *Los Angeles Times*, November 9, 1896, 6, and "In the Prohibited City," *Boston Daily Globe*, January 3, 1897. The structure is known today as the Palace of Earthly Tranquility.

16 Leslie E. Fislar [sic], *Fisler Genealogy*, 1934 (copy at Camden County Historical Society) stated, "According to information given me, the wife of Lorenzo was a Chinese woman, Alena. He went to China as a Photographer and while there was taken seriously ill; [he] was nursed back to health by this woman whom he married after his recovery. I understand that after his marriage they lived for several years in China pending the reconciliation of his family to his marriage, and he brought her back to this country where they lived until their respective deaths."

Quoted by Bennett, 122–23. Census records regarding Alena are inconsistent. The 1900 U.S. Census for Camden recorded that Alena was born in May 1857 and had been married for 28 years, i.e., 1872. The 1905 New Jersey State Census recorded that she was born in June 1859. The 1900 Census stated that the Fislers had no children but the 1910 Census, which implausibly implied that she was born in 1862, recorded that Alena had given birth once but the child was not living. Alena was listed as Mabel, foreign-born, in the 1895 New Jersey State Census, and as Adaline in the 1905 New Jersey State Census.

17 Fisler's return to Camden with a Chinese wife was widely reported in the press. "A Celestial Wife Brought from China by a New Jersey Man," *St. Paul Daily Globe*, June 11, 1884, 6, stated that Mrs. Fisler was educated by an English missionary and was a Methodist Christian. Very petite, "good humored and full of smiles, but withall very reticent...." Her feet were never bound and she spoke English fluently without an accent. The *Watertown (New York), Daily Times*, June 11, 1884, 4, opined that she was the "first real Chinese lady ever seen in this country" but confused Lorenzo with his brother Weston, the baseball player. The *Trenton Evening Times*, June 6, 1884, 4, reported that Fisler had brought home "a novelty in the shape of a Chinese wife."

18 The earliest mention of the partnership was an advertisement in the *Morning Post* (Camden), Sept. 16, 1884, 4: "Fisler & Ganbort [sic], Landscape and Mechanical Photographers, Nos. 712 and 720 Federal street, Camden, N.J. Photographs taken of buildings, boats, groups, machinery and graves, and also mounting and framing of pictures, and all descriptions of out door [sic] photography. Printing for the trade and amateurs. A trial solicited. Prices reasonable." In the 1885 to 1887 directories, they were listed at 511 and 720 Federal, the home addresses of Fisler and Gaubert, respectively. Before and after this partnership, Gaubert was listed as a clerk in Camden directories.

19 "Walt Whitman and Bill Duckett by Lorenzo F. Fisler and Gaubert? ca. October 1886," *The Walt Whitman Archive*, https://whitmanarchive.org/multimedia/zzz.00095.html. The tintypes with the attribution to Fisler are in the collection of Ohio Wesleyan University. Fisler lived around the block from Whitman, lending plausibility to the attribution, but no other tintypes by Fisler have come to my attention.

20 *Morning Post* (Camden), January 6, 1891, 4. Born in New Hampshire in 1841, Ellery J. Hunt had two successive galleries in Camden from 1877 until his death in 1890. He died of cancer of the tongue, reportedly from "incessant pipe smoking." *Photographic Times*, 1891, 45.

21 The advertisement read, "To Photographers, for sale, a lot of photographic negatives of scenes in China and Japan; never published in this country. Apply to L. F. Fisler, 305 Linden St., Camden, N.J." *The Philadelphia Inquirer*,

August 12, 1910, 13.
22 Certificate and Record of Death, New Jersey State Archives. The cause of death was myocarditis with a cystotomy (operation on the bladder) a contributing factor. In his will, dated October 9, 1911, Lorenzo left his entire estate to his wife Alena. Last Will and Testament, D4803, New Jersey State Archives.
23 The Fislers are buried in Section C, Lot 120. Lorenzo's tombstone was moved with him from South Laurel Hill Cemetery. Walter and Abbie Dinmore are also in Evergreen Cemetery, Section O, Lot 295. Evergreen Cemetery records, Camden County Historical Society. The rejection of Alena Fisler by South Laurel Hill Cemetery is in its records; its anti-Chinese exclusion policy is no longer in effect.
24 Civil War Draft Registrations (Ancestry.com): Andrew Sims, 36, picture framer, born Scotland, living in Middle Ward, Camden, June 1863. The 1865 Camden business directory listed him twice, as photographer and picture framer. It is probable that Sims did not serve in the Civil War. An Andrew J. Sims from Pennsylvania was in Company B, 125th Pennsylvania Regiment, but not the same man as the Sims discussed here.
25 References in the text concerning addresses of Sims' galleries are based on city directories. Mirrors and picture frames: *New Republic* (Camden), March 7, 1868, 3, advertisement, "Photograph Gallery, No. 215 Federal Street, Camden, N.J. A. Sims, Photographer and Picture Frame Manufacturer. Looking Glasses, &c. All work properly finished. Satisfaction given."
26 *Camden Democrat*, August 13, 1870, 3, listed as member, Board of Managers, YMCA. *West Jersey Press* (Camden), March 26, 1873, 7, mentioned as class leader, Third St. Methodist Episcopal Church. *Morning Post* (Camden), March 25, 1879, 1, Sims elected a trustee of the Third Street Methodist Episcopal Church.
27 *Camden Democrat*, October 16, 1875, 4, advertisement, "Four Ferreotypes for 25 Cents. Photographs taken in the best style of the Art, at reasonable rates." *Morning Post* (Camden), January 28, 1878, 2, advertisement, "Large photos and frames, $1.50."
28 Charles Shimer Boyer, *Old Ferries, Camden, New Jersey* (n.p.: privately printed, 1921), 12.
29 *Morning Post* (Camden), March 5, 1879, 1, stating that Charles E. Smith will open a jewelry store at 307 Market, taking up some of the show room of Sims the photographer.
30 Death of John E. B. Sims, June 15, 1890, NJ Deaths & Burials Index (via Ancestry.com). According to his death certificate, John was living at 2007 S. 7th Street, Philadelphia, at the time of his death. For addresses and years of Sims' galleries in Philadelphia, see author's Philadelphia Photographers List at http://saretzky.com/history-of-photography-indexes-to-photographers.html.
31 In 1890, an Andrew Sims was assaulted at his home in Philadelphia, but it has not been determined if this was the photographer. *The Philadelphia Inquirer*, September 17, 1890, 6. If Sims the photographer lived in Philadelphia at that time, he soon returned to Camden.
32 Death notice, *The Philadelphia Inquirer*, November 20, 1917, Andrew Sims, 90, died November 18, husband of late Mary S. Sims. Deaths, Mary Sims, December 10, 1915, 811 Vine St., and Andrew Sims, November 20 [sic], 1917, recorded in First Methodist Episcopal church records. Ancestry.com.
33 The surname is sometimes found as Fern but the more common spelling Fearn is used here.
34 England, Select Marriages, 1538–1973. Ancestry.com.
35 The younger John eventually lived in Camden County as did his parents and brothers. In the 1880 Census, he was a barber in Merchantville and in the 1900 Census, he was a watch repairer in Haddonfield. John was married and had several children with his wife Annie.
36 The 1855 New York Census gives Queens as Frederick's birthplace but as Richmond County in the 1860 Port Richmond Census. Between Frederick and William, sisters Alice A. was born in 1854 and Ida F. in 1856. Another son, Albert, was born in 1863. The 1865 Census in Castleton, Richmond County, lists the father John's occupation as straw-hat presser. Ancestry.com.
37 Fearn's Hospital Ticket, U.S.S. Franklin, Boston, November 6, 1871, gives his residence at time of enlistment as Flushing, Queens, and age in 1871 as 21 years old. Census records concerning Frederick's age are inconsistent: 3 in 1855, 8 in 1860, and 47, born January 1853, in the 1900 Census. His second marriage record, July 21, 1884, listed his age as 30 and his death record implied that he was born in 1855. Fearn likely lowered his age when he married his much younger second wife. Ancestry.com.
38 1870 U.S. Census, Middletown, Richmond County, New York. The father John is listed as 40 years old and his wife Amelia (oddly listed as Mary), 41, with children Alice, Ida, William, and Albert. Ancestry.com.
39 Lauren Young, "The Real Electric Frankenstein Experiments of the 1800s," https://www.atlasobscura.com/articles/the-real-electric-frankenstein-experiments-of-the-1800s. Address: Camden city directories, 1875, et seq. By the 1880 Census, John and Amelia had been joined by Amelia's father, John Hearn, 82, but none of their children were living with them.
40 Beginning in 1879, advertisements with testimonials began appearing that extolled the treatment offered by Mrs. A. A. Fearn, Herbalist and Medical Electrician. At least one advertisement mentions that Mr. Fearn also administered a treatment. Among the testimonials, Mrs. Mary Stone stated that she was cured of "womb disease and ulcers." Charles W. Stetser went to Mrs. Fearn for rheumatism and was informed that he also had lung and kidney disease, but she cured him in ten treatments. Mrs.

Terrence Johnson wrote that she was cured of dropsy in an advertisement claiming, "All diseases of women cured." Samuel H. Severns claimed that Mrs. Fearn cured his daughter, age 19, of fits that lasted three days at a time, after 18 treatments. Mrs. R. Evans stated that Mrs. A. A. Fearn removed her cataracts, and her sight was restored in five weeks. That advertisement also mentioned that Mrs. Fearn was selling her Herb Medicine for Dyspepsia and Liver Complaint for 75 cents a bottle. *Morning Post* (Camden), May 24, 1879, 3; August 27, 1879, 3; February 5, 1880, 3; March 29, 1880, 3; November 20, 1880, 4.

41 *Morning Post* (Camden), April 23, 1881, 1.

42 December 5, 1883, 4. Amelia was awarded a patent on July 20, 1886, for her "Life-Preserving Corset," #345,960. The corset featured stays made of cork. Filed March 6, 1886. *Official Gazette of the United States Patent Office*, Volume 36, 1887, 311.

43 *Morning Post* (Camden), October 15, 1884, 1; *The Philadelphia Inquirer*, October 15, 1884, 3.

44 In 1888, the *Morning Post* (Camden) reported that Amelia had been appointed executor of John's estate by the Surrogate in Camden, July 27, 1888, 1. Fearn v. West Jersey Ferry Co., *Pittsburgh Legal Journal*, Number 22, 1891, 196–97; *Pennsylvania State Reports Containing Cases Adjudged in the Supreme Court of Pennsylvania by Boyd Brumrine, State Reporter, Containing Cases Decided at January Term and October Term 1891* (New York and Albany: Bank & Brothers, 1892), 122–29.

45 January 28, 1878, 3; January 29, 1878, 3.

46 *Camden City Directory*, 1878, living at 434 Hamilton Street. In 1879, William lived at 4413 Bridge Avenue.

47 September 20, 1879.

48 1880 Census, Nashville, Davidson County, Tennessee. Schleier was a Prussian-born American photographer, inventor, and diplomat who served as U.S. Consul to Amsterdam, 1890–1893. He pioneered electrical lighting systems for photography studios.

49 *Camden City Directory*, 1882, living at 827 Carpenter Street.

50 Smith kept the Camden location for about a year and in turn was succeeded by Samuel C. Chester, who remained there until 1924. Smith also worked in Hightstown in 1875.

51 See, for example, advertisements, June 4 and August 19, 1885.

52 See, for example, March 8, 1887, 4. Some of the advertisements erroneously listed him as W. B. Fearn instead of W. R. Fearn.

53 City directories for Camden and Glendale. William and Lucy Ziegler briefly lived in Long Beach in 1923 before joining William and Anna Fearn in Glendale at 405 E. Elk Avenue. William and Lucy continued living there with Anna into the 1930s and Anna was still there in 1940.

54 Before Lucy, born in 1882, they had Howard, who was listed as a 21-year-old upholsterer in the 1900 U.S. Census, Camden, Camden County, which listed the William Fearn family at 129 Centre Street. In addition to William and Anna, who was born in February 1859, and the two children, Anna's mother Rebecca Fox, 61, and Anna's brother, Albert F. Fox, 21, lived with the family.

55 1880 U.S. Census, Camden, Camden County. Ancestry.com.

56 New Jersey Death Record, New Jersey State Archives. Annie was buried in Camden Cemetery. Her father's name was John Lawrence on the death record; her mother's name was not noted. Birth of Pansey: New Jersey Birth Record, New Jersey State Archives, October 17, 1883, at 594 Carman Street, Camden. Pansey probably did not survive, as no further mention of her has been found.

57 New Jersey Marriage Record, New Jersey State Archives. It was Georgianna's first marriage and Frederick's second. Her parents were J. Reed and Sallie A. Williams.

58 Marriage: *Camden County Courier*, July 26, 1884, 3. Bertha was born August 1884, according to 1900 U.S. Census, Trenton. Georgianna's age is listed as 30, so she would have been 14 in 1884 but 16 according to her death certificate (see note 75).

59 *Camden Daily Courier*, October 13–16, 19–20, 26–27, 1886, all page 1; *Monmouth Inquirer*, October 21, 1886, 3; in the Atlantic en route to Shanghai: *The Philadelphia Inquirer*, October 18, 1886, 7.

60 One child was Clifford Fred Fearn, born May 1890 in Philadelphia, according to the 1900 U.S. Census, Trenton, although his draft registration card in 1917 gave his birth as May 6, 1889. Ancestry.com. The others were Clarence Fearn, December 17, 1887, born at 586 Benson St., Camden, second child of this marriage, both living; Dora E., October 23, 1892, 315 Perry St., Trenton, fourth child of this marriage, all living; and female [Lorraine], November 30, 1895, 276 Bellevue Ave., Trenton, 5th child, all living. Birth records, New Jersey State Archives.

61 The street name changed from Greene to S. Broad in November 1889. At the same location from 1889 to 1892 was the branch gallery of the prominent photographer James R. Applegate, based in Philadelphia. It has not been determined if there was a business connection between Fearn and Applegate. Applegate was arrested on January 28, 1892, in Philadelphia for running a disorderly house. For Applegate, see the author's "Nineteenth-Century New Jersey Photographers," *New Jersey History*, 122:3–4 (Fall/Winter 2004), 36–143, revised text without illustrations at http://www.gary.saretzky.com/photohistory/resources/photo_in_nj_July_2010.pdf.

62 *Trenton Times*, April 12, 1890, 1.

63 Amelia Fearn was listed in the 1890 *Trenton City Directory* as A. A. Fearn, medical technician, with home at 234 Perry Street and in 1891 with both business and home at 240 E. State Street. Frederick first appears in the

Trenton City Directory in 1891 at 23 S. Broad with home at 315 Perry Street.

64 See, for example, *Trenton Evening Times*, March 8, 1891, 4. Amelia is listed in the 1891 *Trenton City Directory* as an electrician with the same home address.

65 For example, *Trenton Evening Times*, November 22, 1895, 4.

66 See the author's "Last Man Standing: E. S. Dunshee, Veteran Trenton Photographer," *Garden State Legacy*, Issue 30, December 30, 2015. http://www.GardenStateLegacy.com.

67 *Trenton Evening Times*, Jan. 31, 1899, 5. One dollar in 1899 was worth about $31.35 in 2020 dollars.

68 *Trenton Evening Times*, December 19, 1900, 1.

69 *Trenton Evening Times*, January 15, 1901, 1. The paper reported the name erroneously as Eetta.

70 *Trenton Evening Times*, July 22, 1901, 5.

71 One of the girls was Dora, who had appeared as "Baby" Fearn in several theatrical performances. The other was Lorraine. *Trenton Evening Times*, April 29, 1903, 1.

72 *Trenton Evening Times*, March 19, 1904, 2; New Jersey Death Record.

73 Civil War Pension Index, 1861–1934. Ancestry.com. Frederick had applied previously for an pension as an invalid on July 11, 1901. His naval rank was Landsman in the application.

74 New Jersey Marriage Index, 1901–2016 and birth of Arthur in New Jersey, U.S. United Methodist Church Records, 1800–1970. Ancestry.com. 1910 U.S. Census, Philadelphia, Geoergianna, 43, with James W. Hickey, 36, bricklayer, no children present. 1915 N.J. Census, Atlantic City, Georgianna, age not given, with James, 43, her daughters Lorraine, 18 and Etta, 14, and son, Arthur, 4. The daughters' surname was recorded as Hickey so they may have been adopted. In the 1920 U.S. Census, Atlantic City, Georgianna, 53, born Maryland, was recorded with husband James W. Hickey, 45, born England, home builder, emigrated 1896, with son Arthur, 9, and daughter Lorraine, 23. In the 1930 U.S. Census, Atlantic City, Georgianna, 62, was listed with James, 55, building contractor, and their son Arthur, 19, a musician in an orchestra.

75 New Jersey Deaths and Burials Index, 1798–1971. ancestry.com.

76 Carolyn Weigel, Archivist, Ursinus College, email to author, January 13, 2021. Frank's older brother Eugene also attended in 1871–1872.

77 The *Courier-Post* (Camden), November 17, 1898, 1.

78 December 8, 1901, 24.

79 Constance McCabe, ed., *Platinum and Palladium Photographs: Technical History, Connoisseurship and Preservation* (Washington, DC: American Institute for Conservation, 2017).

80 The *Courier Post*, July 3, 1902, 2. As a good citizen, in August 1905, Edward Sherman identified a man standing outside a jewelry store near his studio, shortly before it was robbed. Two men distracted the storekeeper and a third ran out with a tray with thirty diamond rings worth $1,000. The three were arrested shortly thereafter but only the one who took the jewels was charged and the other two released. The Thomas Smedley & Son jewelry store was at 920 Broadway, near the Sherman's South Studio at 934 Broadway. Police later arrested a woman who was mailed a ring by the thief. "$1000 Worth of Diamonds . . . 3 Colored Men Under Arrest," *Morning Post* (Camden), August 2, 1905, 1; "Thief Made Haul of Diamonds in Camden," *The Philadelphia Inquirer*, August 3, 1905, 3; "Held for Diamond Theft," *The Philadelphia Inquirer*, August 4, 1905, 3; *Morning Post*, September 18, 1905, 1.

81 *Camden-Post Telegram*, August 20, 1902, 3. See also *Courier-Post*, August 20, 1902, 1; *The Philadelphia Inquirer*, August 21, 1902, 4. The *Camden-Post Telegram* is indexed as *Courier-Post* in Newspapers.com.

82 *Courier-Post*, June 24, 1904, 11. This synopsis omits Sherman's efforts to assure the public of the couple's dedication and well-deserved reputation for superior work. Sherman's claim in this announcement regarding priority in the use of electric illumination before Philadelphia photographers is rather doubtful considering the significant number of studios there. In the United States, photographer William Kurtz of New York perhaps was the first to specialize in electric lighting in the fall of 1882, although it was not widely adopted until the early 1900s. William Welling, *Photography in America: The Formative Years, 1839–1900: A Documentary History* (New York: Thomas Y. Crowell, 1978), 279. See also note 48. In the early 1900s, the Shermans also had a studio in Burlington, as evidenced by a cabinet card with both Camden and Burlington in the imprint, but were not listed in Burlington directories, so their presence there must have been brief.

83 *Courier-Post*, August 29, 1904, 9.

84 *Camden, New Jersey: The City's Rise and Growth. Commercial and Manufacturing Advantages. Its Future Possibilities* (Philadelphia: Shelden Co., 1904). Copy at the Camden County Historical Society.

85 *Tampa Tribune*, October 17, 1914, 9. In 1922, William Landless managed the Sherman studio at Boardwalk and Cedar Ave. in Wildwood. In 1926, it was managed by Mrs. Margaret L. Rhorer. Wildwood city directories.

86 Jon L. Wilson, "Days of Fear: A Lynching in St. Petersburg," *Tampa Bay History* 5:2 (Fall/Winter 1983), 4-26, available at http://scholarcommons.usf.edu/cgi/viewcontent.cgi?article=3518&context=flstud_pub. There was extensive coverage in local newspapers, including *St. Petersburg Evening Independent, St. Petersburg Daily Times*, and *Tampa Tribune;* only some articles are cited by Wilson. See also "Edward F. Sherman Slain," *Bulletin of Photography* 15 (1914), 656.

87 Mary's subsequent life remains undocumented. Possibly she was Mary C. Sherman, 73, born in Philadelphia,

widow, listed without occupation in the 1940 Census in Gloucester City, Camden County.

88 Among other women photographers of this era who worked in Camden, Henrietta L. Wardle, who partnered with Henry D. Garns, merits particular attention. See list of more than 100 nineteenth-century New Jersey women photographers at http://saretzky.com/history-of-photography-indexes-to-photographers.html. For overviews, see Naomi Rosenblum, *A History of Women Photographers* (Paris, London, & New York: Abbeville Press, 1994); Katherine Manthorne, *Women in the Dark: Female Photographers in the U.S., 1850–1900* (Atglen, PA: Schiffer Publishing, 2020); and Boris Friedewald, *Women Photographers from Julia Margaret Cameron to Cindy Sherman* (Munich, London, and New York: Prestel Publishing, 2018).

Old "Danny" Haulstard and His Humble Dwelling

A Typical Backwoodsman

Old "Danny" and His Home

He is Peaceable, Ignorant and Fond of Telling Stories—A "News" Representative Pays Him a Call.

A representative of the *News* had occasion to visit the Russian Hebrew settlement about one and a half miles north of Norma and while there ran across a full type of genuine backwoodsman. His hovel, hut or whatever it may be called, is a one-story frame building, 10 by 12 in size. It has weather-boards, but no plaster, and a stove pipe sticks out of a window.

It is in a small clearing which is surrounded by water. The *News* man gave a gentle rap and a very welcome "Come in" was the reply. He went in and his first sight was a bunk or bed on one side, made of coats, guano sacks, etc., while on the other side was a stove and cooking utensils. A soap box was handed him and he took a seat.

It was learned that the proprietor was Daniel Haulstard, familiarly known as "Danny." He is very talkative and can relate several good "bear stories," of how he has killed bears years ago in the swamps near the door, but they are all gone now. He says there are still some rattlesnakes "around yere," but he is not much afraid of them.

The greatest story Danny told the reporter was one concerning the time when "a big fire was raging over the world." He says the whole world seemed to be on fire. "I had been to Wineland and wen I cum home the woods all around my place wus all in a far, and my house and two dogs wus all burned up, and I had a lot of money burnt up too, nearly a dollar."

The neighbors say that Danny is very peaceable and willing to help, especially at hog-killing time, and the only pay he asks is a small piece of last year's salt pork.

You can find Danny during camp meeting at some brook along the road, always willing to water horses that come along, and some Sundays he gathers in several pennies. No doubt some of the readers of the *News* remember seeing him last summer, during Malaga camp meeting, somewhere along the road with a bucket in hand. He picks huckleberries, gathers wild grapes and carts wood to Vineland, and may be seen almost any Saturday in Vineland, around the auction sales.

Danny is said to have come from a very well-to-do family, but he and his brother David (now deceased) preferred living in this way.

David died several years ago while at work in Vineland. He had a fit, and persons who were there say that they began to rub his limbs to bring him out of it but before they could get the dirt off he died.

Danny claims to have a good "cete" for making bread. It is: A sack of flour, a bucket of water and a little salt; set it away until it rises and then bake it on top of the stove (cooks, please try it for yourselves). He is uneducated and, like Topsy, does not know how old he is. Some of the neighbors claim that he is 60, while others say 75.

He is never willing to swap horses unless he can give a little boot; then he knows his new horse is better than his old one.

Bridgeton Evening News (Bridgeton, New Jersey), Jan 12, 1898. 3.

George F. Hammond Plumbing Office. Camden born in August 1865, Frank E. Mead, at the surprisingly young age of 22, employed his skills as an architect to design this stunning office building for plumber George F. Hammond in 1888. The 1880 federal decennial Census enumerates Frank, age 14, as an apprentice architect. His father, William, worked as a house carpenter and this likely provided the impetus for Frank to enter an allied field. A paragraph appearing on the front page of the *Camden Daily Courier*, April 25, 1888, edition, states: "George F. Hammond, the plumber, has purchased the Garwood property at the southeast corner of Third street and Taylor avenue. He will build a plumbing shop on the lot adjoining the house, and will occupy the latter as his residence." Hammond commissioned Mead to design the office and it was truly an impressive work of beauty, complete with a gryphon on the façade corner, an incised floral spray containing the date "1888" within a wreath above the windows, and a side dormer with a spire roof. The brickwork appears to be checkerboard Flemish bond, even on the sidewall along Taylor Avenue. Mead designed the primary entry around faux flared columns with capitals featuring exquisite carvings. Leaded glass windows can be seen throughout the building. The building culminates with a gambrel roof over half of the structure and features a very narrow leaded window above the floral spray and wreath. Following this successful design, Frank entered the Pennsylvania Museum and School of Industrial Art in 1889 to study architecture. He then entered partnership arrangements with two firms before leaving the area in 1901, when he relocated to San Diego. Mead died in 1940. The Hammond office building survived until at least 1967, but an urban renewal project between then and 1970 replaced the buildings on South Third Street with a parking lot.

"Big Saturday" in the Pines
The Burlington Gazette, Friday, August 1, 1845

Edmund Morris

We have been wondering for the last four weeks, what in the world could be the meaning of some six to a dozen large four horse stages, crowded with passengers, driving daily through our streets from the wharf into the interior of the country. Besides the passengers aforesaid, we remarked great quantities of mammoth travelling trunks, guns, dogs, &c. together with an absurd collection of band-boxes, the latter generally in proportion to the number of female passengers. Multitudes of these things were piled on the stage top, where also, the driver was frequently perched, having been driven to a seat above by the press of passengers below. On enquiring as to where this multitude of people could be going, some persons mentioned "Greenwood," others said "Brown's Mills"; but as neither of these places is marked down even on the latest edition of the map of New Jersey, we rested content with a very slender amount of information on the subject. A fortunate circumstance, however, has completely illuminated us as to the mysterious movements of these people.

On Saturday last, while seated at our desk, having just commenced an editorial article which we feel certain would have electrified our readers, but which they may very shortly look for, three good friends drove up to our office door, and invited us to make a fourth passenger in their projected trip to these identical places of Greenwood and Brown's Mills. The thing was irresistible—we dropped the pen—and taking a seat with two aldermen and one judge, left behind us for a whole day, the plagues of proof sheets and of editorials.

After a ride of some two hours through the rich and highly cultivated country which lies back of Burlington, we drove up to the hotel door in Pemberton. This was near ten o'clock—yet already the whole world of New Jersey seemed moving. Carriage after carriage drove by, turning off at the road by the County House on their way to Greenwood and the Mills, and loaded with sprucely dressed beaux, with girls in white dresses, pink ribbons and green veils, who seemed not only to laugh, but to grow fat amid the clouds of dust which ever and anon rose up on either side of the road. These vehicles were of all descriptions, from the light trotting-sulkey down to the canvass covered farm wagon, the former carrying the fashionable buck of the township, the latter jammed with the man having a wife and thirteen children, all on their patient way to spend the day at Greenwood and the Mills. These symptoms of a great gathering were abundantly realised as we plunged into the tall pine forest which surrounded the Greenwood boarding house. Here we alighted, and securing our horses in the woods, began our observations on a succession of scenes which were entirely new to us.

Greenwood is a large shingle palace, standing solitary and alone, just in the edge of the Pines, about twenty miles from Burlington, at the termination of the Kinkora railroad. This road was built by a company for

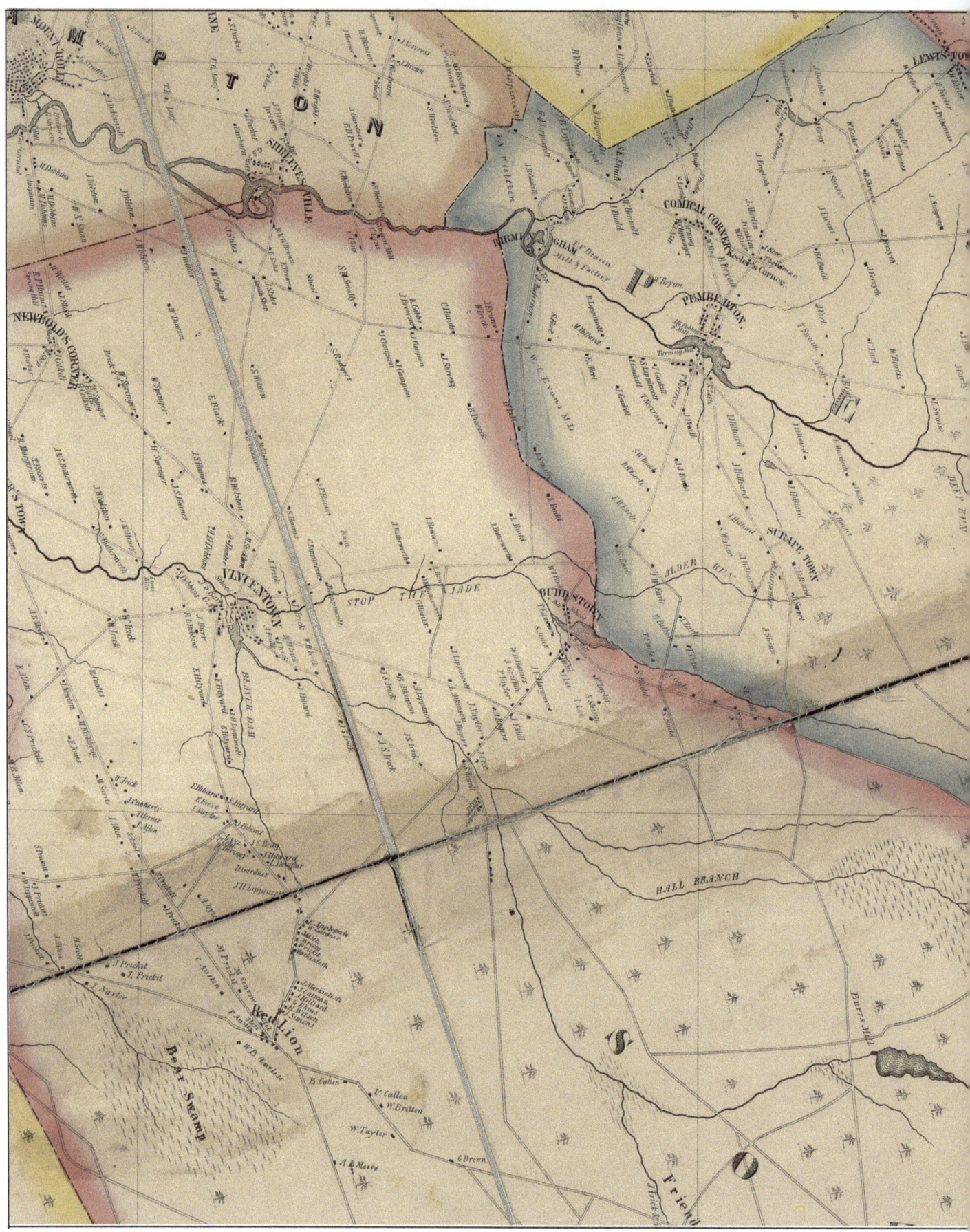

"Big Saturday" in the Pines

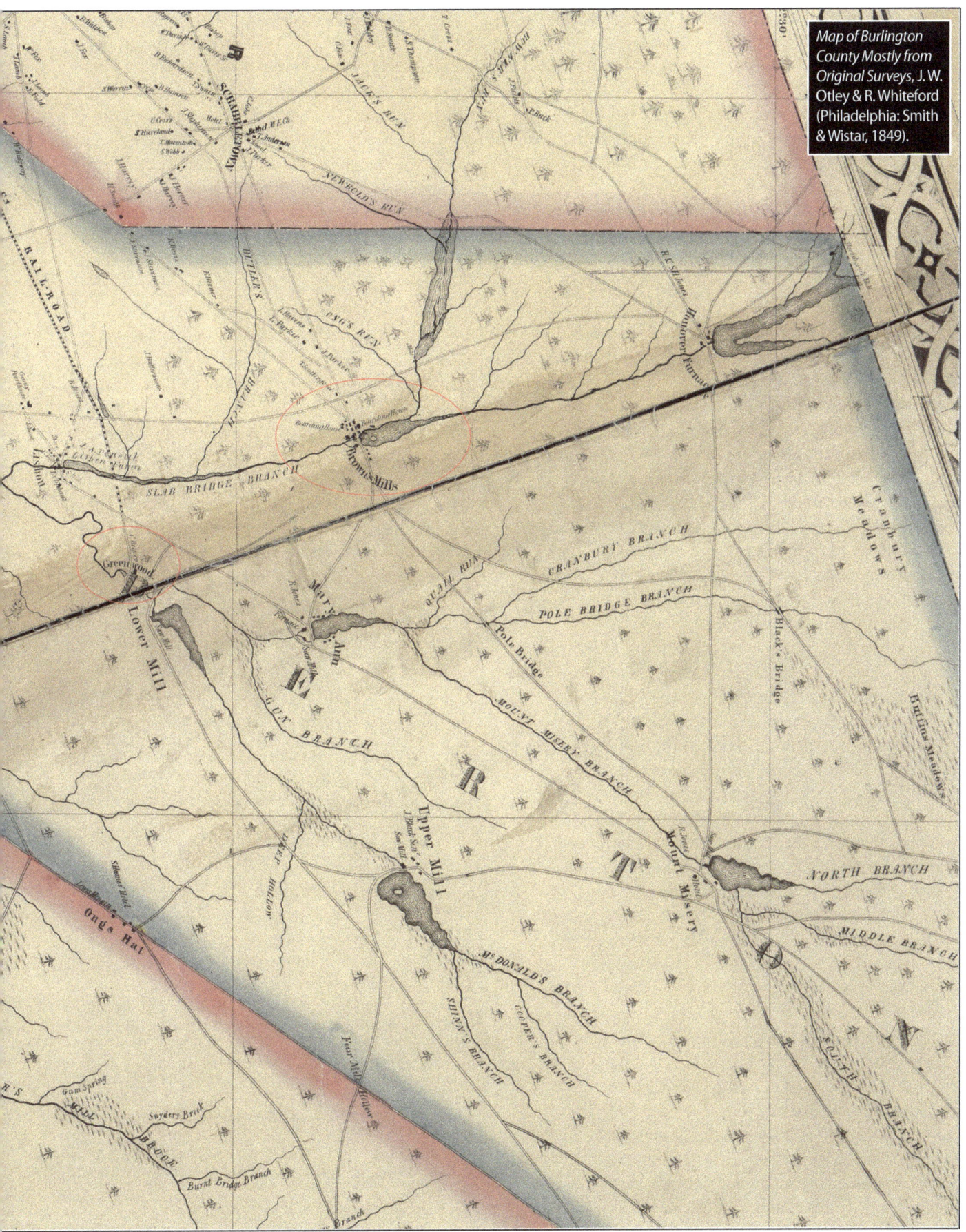

Map of Burlington County Mostly from Original Surveys, J. W. Otley & R. Whiteford (Philadelphia: Smith & Wistar, 1849).

the purpose of bringing into market the vast quantities of pine timber which had long been comparatively valueless, owing to its distance from market. It commences on the Delaware below Bordentown, and stretches up into a body of magnificent timber, whose tall trunks rise up without a single limb to the height of thirty and forty feet. Much of this has been cut off and taken to market over the railroad, but thousands of acres yet remain untouched. The railroad, however, from causes we are not acquainted with, has proved a disastrous speculation, inasmuch as the benign agency of the sheriff has recently been called in to decide the question of ownership.

The Greenwood House was built when speculation was busy in predicting the future increase of the place. Now, speculation being dead and buried, it is devoted to the entertainment of summer boarders from the large cities, who flock in crowds to breathe the healthful and hunger-breeding air of the Pines. A good table is kept by the proprietor, and numerous waiters are every thing, in the way of attention, that could be desired. Greenwood has now about sixty boarders, assembled from all parts of the adjoining states, who pass their time pleasantly enough, in conversation, eating, sleeping, bathing in a branch of the Rancocas near at hand, and—walking in the sand.

Leaving the house, you walk a hundred yards into the woods, where the peculiar tastes of Jerseymen are strikingly displayed. Here were two ten pin alleys, crowded with players and lookers on. Between them stood a long, roughly built shell of pine boards, used for dancing. The sound of the fiddle, and the shuffling of many feet, indicated that dancing had already begun; and such was the energy of the Jersey girls, that we were in continual alarm for the safety of their bustles. For aught we know they may be dancing at this very moment. In the woods surrounding these houses, we counted nearly sixty carriages! After dinner there was a general moving off to Brown's Mills, some three miles further, the road being clear white sand, winding over stumps and bushes, and presenting on either side, traces of the recent destructive fires which have traversed over these regions, coming within a quarter of a mile of Greenwood itself.

But if Greenwood presented a lively scene, Brown's Mills exceeded it in every way. Here five times the number of visitors were assembled. The woods were fairly jammed with wagons of all kinds, probably two or three hundred being scattered about wherever there was an opening to tie the horses. Stalls, or perambulating pie carts, were stationed about in various quarters, at which poor oysters and worse gin were in incessant demand. At least ten to fifteen hundred visitors were on the ground, exclusive of the regular boarders at the two houses at the Mills. Here also were two ten pin alleys and two dancing houses—all built of the roughest boards in the roughest manner possible, and all crowded with players and dancers, the latter having barely room to exercise their legs among the shins of the admiring crowd which pressed around them on every side. Even the windows of these dancing rooms were packed with gaily dressed girls, looking on with absorbing interest on the scene, and drinking in with high relish, the strains of music which proceeded from the well worn fiddle strings of the great stimulator of the dance. The dancing was carried on with true republican independence. Some of the gentlemen danced in boots and hats, some without coats, and many of the girls with bonnets and veils.

The idea occurred to us (about dinner time), how was this enormous assemblage of people to be fed? So taking a turn in the rear of the kitchen, we noticed the most extensive gastronomic preparations. One group of four women were engaged exclusively in splitting a

BROWN'S MILLS, N. J.—THE HORNER House having been refitted is again open for the reception of boarders at this well-known summer resort. This place is unsurpassed for health, having the renovating pine breeze and the air off a beautiful lake.
Accessible by Camden, Pemberton and Hightstown Railroad to Wrightstown, thence by daily stage four miles to Brown's Mills. Passengers take the 4 o'clock boat, foot of Market street. JOHN HORNER, Proprietor.

COUNTRY BOARD—HIGHLAND DELL House.—This house, capable of accommodating one hundred boarders, is situated in the mountains of Pennsylvania, ninety miles from the city of New York, one hundred miles from Philadelphia, and one and-a-half miles from Stroudsburg. Two daily trains, leaving Kensington depot at 7 o'clock A. M. and 3½ P. M., leaving New York city 8 o'clock A. M. and 4 P. M. Large farm attached, which supplies this house with fresh vegetables, butter, eggs, milk, &c. Livery attached. Carriages at Stroudsburg depot to meet the trains. For further information, apply to CHARLES FOULKE, Stroudsburg, Monroe county, Pa.

BROWN'S MILLS BOARDING HOUSE, originally kept by the Brown family, is now open for the reception of permanent and transient Boarders. The beautiful lake, the boats thereon, the fishing, the bathing, the delightful medicated mineral springs, the renovating pine breeze, the promenading in the splendid groves of lofty pines, all contribute to make the place heathful for invalids, and delightful to those seeking comfort and pleasure. Passengers take the 4 o'clock boat, foot of Market Street Wharf, to Camden, thence by cars by the way of Moorestown, Mount Holly, Pemberton, to Wrightston, where stages will be in readiness to convey passengers to Brown's Mills.
THOMAS SCATTERGOOD, Proprietor of Boarding House; JOHN HORNER, Proprietor of Stages.

DOUBLING GAP, WHITE SULPHUR AND Chalybeate Springs, thirty miles west of Harrisburg,

The Philadelphia Inquirer, July 18, 1868.

"Big Saturday" in the Pines

pile of chickens down the back, previous to bedevilling them. As the Romans counted the number of their enemies slain in battle, by the bushels of rings they gathered from their fingers, so did we estimate the quantity of dead poultry; for in one single pile we saw a bushel of gizzards. But ample preparations had been made: for it seems that this practice of assembling at these places has long been fashionable among Jerseymen, and the company was therefore expected. In July, after the harvest is fairly in, the farmers meet by common understanding, every Saturday in that month, to spend the day in the Pines. As the month advances, so the congregation increases, and the last Saturday is known as the "big Saturday." After that the company thins off. It happened, therefore, that we were witnesses of the orgies of the "big-Saturday." Almost every part of the state was represented. There were whole families from Salem; trains of wagons from Monmouth; delegates from Trenton; bright faces from Camden; and the number of Burlington folks which we met at every turn, kept us in a state of continual surprise. Altogether, it was such a scene as we never before witnessed.

Browns Mill's has long been celebrated as a summer retreat. There are now about one hundred boarders at the two houses. They constitute a highly respectable community; and though drawn from several distant States, yet the society enjoyed among them is singularly agreeable, in which intelligence, refined manners, and a disposition to be sociable and pleasant with each other, mingled with the charms of female society, renders this solitary dwelling place in the Pines a most delightful summer resort. The air of the Pines—the water—the absence from the perplexities of business—the perfect relaxation of the mind—added to the good fare and polite attention of the hosts—are found to be highly beneficial to the inmates. They of course have no connection with the swarms of "big Saturday" visitors; but on these great occasions quietly yield the ground for them, and from the loop holes of their retreat look on with amazement at the scenes presented by this great assemblage.

As night approached, we left on our homeward journey: but we understand the evening scene is much more lively than that during the day. Fires are then lighted up on platforms raised some ten feet from the ground, in various places through the woods, and dancing rages with a perfect furor. So great is this passion for dancing, that as we stopped at Wrightstown on our way home, we found the same amusement carried on at both the public houses there. In one of them, there was dancing in three rooms at the same time, all to the sound of one fiddle; now and then a girl was carried out, exhausted by the heat and exertion, but a fresh hand supplied her place, and the sport went on without interruption. In addition to this, a fight sprung up in the bar-room, but was speedily suppressed. Finally the night was pitch dark and rainy. Several wagons were upset in the road, the drivers being unable to discern the track: and from what we saw of these upsets, we are quite sure that some of the girls do not believe a harvest home in the Pines is what it has been cracked up to be.

Our own opinion is that a deplorable school of morals is opened by these annual gatherings. As multitudes of young men and girls participate in them, we can readily understand how fatal they must be to the temperance, sobriety, and chastity of some who go into them even with the best intentions.

This piece was originally published in *The Burlington Gazette*, August 1, 1845. The text was proofread and edited by Sierra Estremera, Stockton Class of 2021, who is graduating with a degree in creative writing. Sierra hopes to continue her editing work for publishing companies and eventually to have one of her own novels published.

In the Woods, Mill Road in the Cedars, Lower Bank, Burlington County, c. 1906. Here a well-dressed young woman, perhaps a summertime visitor, stands beside horse and buggy. She is out for a ride in the Pines. Courtesy of the Paul W. Schopp Collection.

The Skinny on the Privy:
Investigation of the Shipman Mansion Privy

John W. Lawrence

Since 2016, the Shipman Mansion Foundation (the Foundation) has been engaged in restoring the Shipman Mansion, an imposing Second Empire, three-story, slate mansard roofed dwelling overlooking the Delaware River in Edgewater Park, Burlington County (photograph 1). Since 1922, the building has served as home to the Red Dragon Canoe Club (RDCC), the second oldest, continually operating boat club in the United States. The mansion building and several outbuildings on six acres of land were placed in the New Jersey and National Registers of Historic Places in 2000 and 2001, respectively.

As part of the ongoing restoration of this property, the Foundation received a grant from New Jersey Cultural Trust (NJCT) in 2017 to restore one of the more notable outbuildings on the property: the privy. According to older members of the canoe club, the privy remained serviceable into the 1980s, but by the first decade of the twenty-first century was little more than an imploding heap of timber shrouded in plastic in a heroic attempt to preserve what little was left of the structure (photograph 2). When we embarked on the project, we had little notion of what in fact could be salvaged of the original building.

Photograph 1. The 1870 Shipman Mansion, looking south from Delaware River.

Photograph 2. The Shipman Mansion privy prior to restoration, looking west.

There were other important historical questions about this structure. Naturally, being what it is, the privy did not appear in any written history of the property or the canoe club and nothing was known with certitude about its origins. There was an enigma to the structure as well. It was known to be a "five-holer" with separate entrance doors for men and women on opposite sides of the building (photograph 3). It was also known that the couple who built the mansion circa 1870, Paul and Alice Shipman, had occupied the property until their demise in 1917 but never had children.[1] Newspaper accounts contemporaneous to the time of their death suggest that they were not socially engaged with the local community[2] and if they were not pronounced socialites, why would they need a five-hole privy? Despite the grandeur of the mansion, the Shipmans were not particularly wealthy.[3] The possibility existed that the RDCC, with its numerous members and active social activities, could have had the privy built sometime after they purchased the property in 1922, but it seemed an anachronism to be building privies in the 1920s, when indoor plumbing had become common in middle- and upper-class suburban households. In fact, documents related to the sale of the mansion indicate that a bathroom had already been installed there by the time the club purchased it from the Shipmans' heirs.[4] In sum, who had built this privy and why were a mystery.

These questions notwithstanding, privies as a "special function" type of human structure have always been of great interest to archaeologists for the stories they can tell about their original users and the times in which they lived. There are two reasons for this. First, as waste receptacles, most privies were used to dispose of all kinds of domestic items, not just human waste. They are therefore apt to contain the panoply of household items its members used. These "small things forgotten" are in turn a rich source for the archaeologist's interpre-

The Skinny on the Privy

Photograph 3. Restored seats on the women's side of the privy. Note the child-sized seat.

structural elements from the site, salvage intact elements, and reconstruct the privy keeping to the original design and materials as closely as possible. The archaeological investigation consisted of two phases, a non-invasive remote sensing survey of the area surrounding the privy (which included a metal detector), and a traditional archaeological excavation of the privy vault. To avoid the problem of encountering unnecessary "noise" in the form of metal hardware that might be scattered around the outside of the privy by its disassembly, the remote sensing survey was done prior to any other site work. The archaeological excavation was carried out once the structural remains were removed and the privy vault exposed.

tation of what life was like in the past. Second, many privy vaults (particularly colonial era) took the form of shafts dug deep into the surrounding soils and were at times lined with wood to avoid collapse. As confined spaces, these shafts by and large would preserve the sequence in which waste was deposited into the privy and thereby prevent an immoderate degree of "mixing" that is the bane of archaeologists whose first job is to disentangle the continuum of material culture in any soil deposits into discrete time periods.

With these facts in mind, the NJHT recommended that the Foundation engage in an archaeological investigation of the privy as part of the restoration process, and the fieldwork was conducted in coordination with the efforts of the firm of *Long Neck Partners*, who were hired to remove the existing

THE REMOTE SENSING SURVEY

The remote sensing portion of the overall archaeological investigation employed three different remote sensing devices, a Ground-Penetrating Radar (GPR) device, an Electro-Magnetic (EM) sensing device; and a metal detector (photograph 4). Cleared space around

Photograph 4. Mr. Robert Wiencek operating the ground-penetrating radar.

the privy structure was not great due to the presence of other structures and dense vegetation; ultimately an area some 40 feet (north-south) by 50 feet (east-west) was tested in this remote sensing phase of the investigation (figure 1). Mr. Robert Wiencek and Paul McLeod of EPI, Inc. conducted the remote sensing survey.

The metal detecting survey of the privy area discovered a large amount of modern trash (e.g., foil, pull-tabs, bottle caps, etc.). These items are undoubtedly the result of the area along the east side of the privy having been used for garbage storage by the RDCC for over the past 20 years. These finds were for the most part not recorded nor collected. However, several finds not associated with modern club trash were detected by the metal detector. These included recent vintage coins, fasteners (nails, washers, sockets), a broken silver finger ring, and the most intriguing item, a brass, ½-inch round "ball" or "Zouave" button.

These objects were encountered within a few inches of the ground surface to the north and east of the privy (figure 1). Of all the artifacts, only the brass button is considered historic and possibly dates to the period of Shipman occupation, if not earlier (photograph 5). The "ball" button was a characteristic element of the uniforms worn by Zouave units formed in both the North and South during the Civil War. Named after Algerian troops in the French Army in North Africa, these volunteer light infantry militia units could be recognized by their colorful and distinctive uniforms, which included baggy pantaloons, sash, and short jacket that sported the distinctive metallic "ball" buttons (figure 2). (These troops would also sometimes wear a fez, complete with tassel.) Zouve-inspired jackets also became popular as an item of women's apparel during the Civil War, but don't appear to have used the same type of buttons. Zouave regiments from Northern states gradually vanished from the U.S. military in the 1870s and 1880s, or about the time that the Shipman Mansion was built and later occupied by Paul R. Shipman and his wife, Alice.

Neither Paul R. Shipman nor his wife Alice are known to have had connections with any military units —Zouave or otherwise—during or after the Civil War.[5] In fact, Paul Shipman is credited with helping to keep Kentucky neutral during that fratricidal conflict. Both Shipmans had connections to President Lincoln's family and associates, but no known association with infantry troops on either side of the conflict. The presence of this military-type button on the RDCC property is therefore enigmatic and cannot be connected to the Shipman or any other occupants of the Shipman Mansion. Zouave units were raised in both New Jersey (such as the "West Jersey Zouaves") and Pennsylvania, and the button may have been lost by a member of one of these regiments, perhaps during mobilization. The Edgewater Wharf had been constructed at the foot of Edgewater Avenue prior to the Civil War and may have been a transshipment point during troop movements.[6]

Figure 2. Pvt. Francis E. Brownell, 11th N.Y. Regt. in Zouave uniform; note jacket buttons. Courtesy of the Library of Congress.

Photograph 5. Brass "ball" button for Zouave uniform.

The Skinny on the Privy

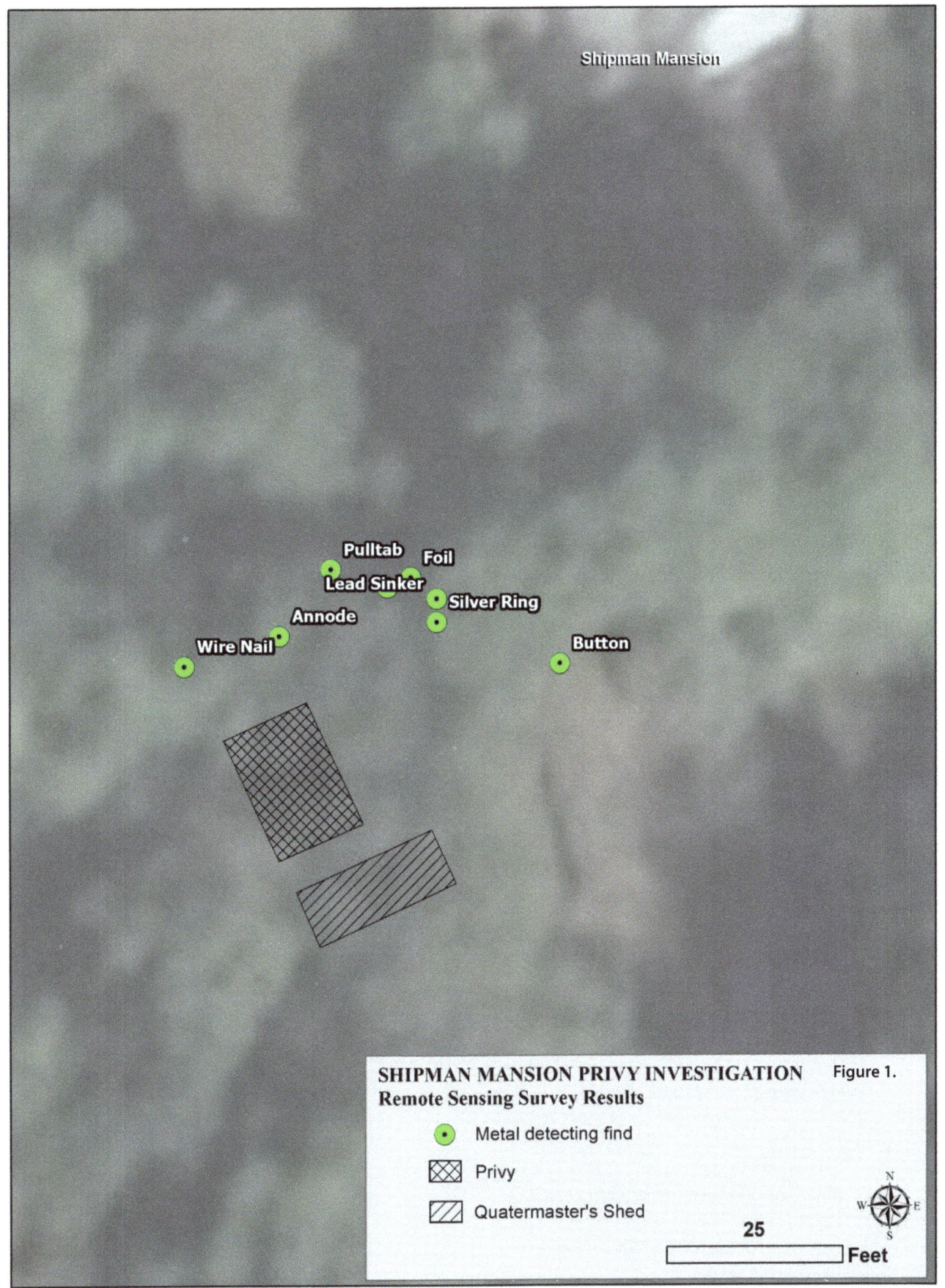

SoJourn

Photograph 6. Shipman Mansion privy after surface cleaning, looking south. Unexcavated brick privy vault in center, brick piers visible at corners. Note groundhog hole along the northern wall of the privy vault. The cement panels surrounded the structure are not part of the original construction, they were placed at some undetermined time in the last 50 years or so.

The Archaeological Investigation

Once the site had been cleared of surficial debris, it was found to consist of the following features (photograph 6; figure 3):

- Four brick piers underlay each corner of the structure;
- A central, brick lined privy pit or vault was located at the center of the structure;
- Use of roofing slate as shims between the top of the brick pillars and remnant wooden sills resting on top of the brick;
- Two courses of cement slabs had been placed around the exterior of the privy building by members of the RDCC, which is not part of the original construction. These have subsequently been removed from the site as not part of its historic fabric.

The Piers. The piers were generally similar in construction and consisted of three courses of four bricks at each corner; only the top course appeared to have been originally mortared, the remainder were dry-laid. The mortar, however, was to a large extent missing and the bricks somewhat disarticulated.[7]

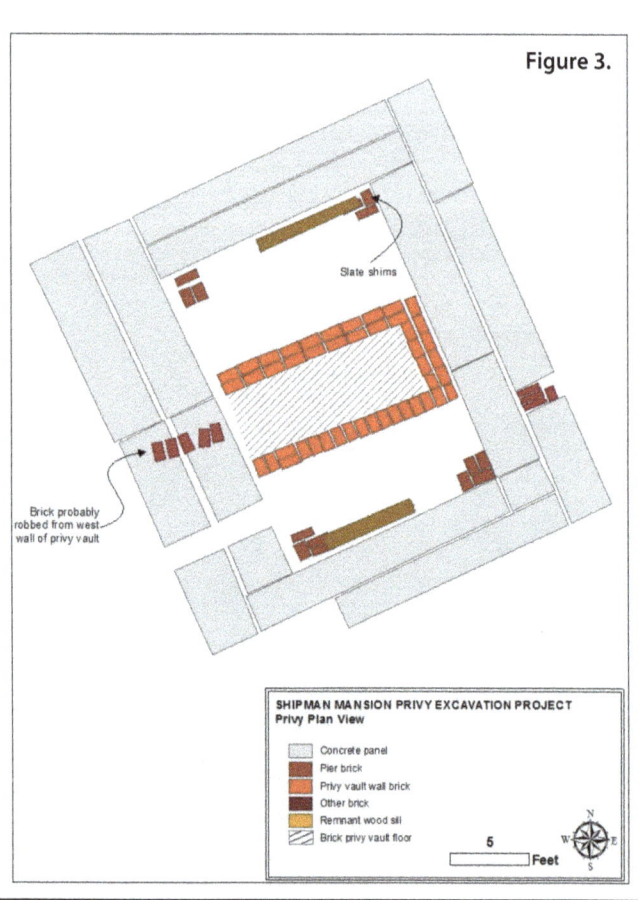

Figure 3.

38

The Skinny on the Privy

The Privy Vault. This is a four-foot (north-south) wide by 6.25 feet long (east-west) by 13-inch-deep brick lined open "box" that crosses the central core of the privy interior. The privy pit formed a common receptacle for both the men's and women's side of the privy. According to Mr. Blaetz of *Long Neck Partners*,[8] the interior dividing wall of the privy only extended to the top course of the vault brick and was open between wall studs. This design would have allowed odors from the privy pit to vent upward through the wall, to vent out through the open roof structure.

The privy vault itself was box-shaped, constructed of either a single line of brick laid north-south, or a double-line of brick laid perpendicularly; the overall effect was to create north and south walls of uniform width (8 inches) (photograph 7). The floor of the privy was made of a double course of flat, un-mortared brick; the vault was nine inches deep, from the top of the brick walls to the top of the floor. A double line of brick oriented north-south formed the 8-inch-wide east wall of vault. The walls were four courses high, attaining a level elevation with the four corner piers and thereby providing structural support to the wooden super-structure. There was no corresponding brick west wall to the privy vault. This area corresponded to the "clean out" door on the exterior of the privy (photograph 8). We speculate that although some brick may have been robbed from this area, this side of the vault did not have a full wall matching the east side, which would have prevented access to the privy pit for the purposes of periodically cleaning it out.

Shims. At both the northeast and southwest corners, pieces of roofing slate had been placed between the top of the brick and remnants of the original wooden sill still *in situ* (photograph 9). The use of roofing slate as a shim suggests the contemporaneity of

Photograph 7. Excavated brick privy vault, looking north. "Robbed" bricks from west wall in bottom left hand corner of photograph.

Photograph 8. West (back) side of privy. Hinged "clean out" door just visible base of wall behind center cinder block.

Photograph 9. Northeastern privy pier. Note the two pieces of roofing slate (bottom corner) used as shims.

Table 1. Catalog of artifacts recovered from the Shipman Mansion privy vault.

	South (women's half)				North (men's half)			
	Count	Material	Color	Item	Count	Material	Color	Item
Level 1 (0-3" below surface)	1	Plastic	White	Fork	1	Plastic	White	12" diameter Styrofoam plate fragment
	1	Plastic	White	Tampon applicator	1	Plastic/brass	Red/brass	Spent shotgun shell, marked "BLANK"
	1	Plastic	White	Nylon panties	1	Bone	N/A	medium mammal rib bone fragment
					1	Glass	Green	Bottle neck and lip
					1	Glass	Medium brown	Bottle body fragment
					1	Glass	Transparent	Bottle neck and lip, screw top
					1	Metal	N/A	Bottle cap, highly corroded
					1	Plastic	White	Cigar holder
					1	Plastic	Translucent	Cigarette filter
					2	Metal	N/A	Highly corroded tin can fragments
Level 2 (3-6" below surface)	1	Wood	N/A	Toilet paper roll holder	1	Bone	N/A	Large mammal, vertebra, sawn
	1	Glass	Transparent	Medicine bottle neck and lip	3	Bone	N/A	Small mammal or bird, unidentified
	1	Bone	N/A	Large mammal long bone condyle	1	Plastic	White	Condom fragment
					3	Glass	Medium brown	Bottle body fragments
					1	Coal	Black	Fragment, unburned
					1	Rubber	White	Tangle of string, baseball wrapping?
					1	Glass	N/A	Burned glob
					2	Metal	N/A	Bottle cap, rubber gasket
					2	Metal	N/A	Unidentified corroded pieces of sheet metal, flat
					1	Bone	N/A	Large mammal, vertabra, sawn

the privy structure with the Shipman Mansion, which is believed to have been completed by 1870. The mansion was constructed with a slate mansard roof.

Privy hardware. Restoration of the salvageable elements to the privy structure for reinstallation on the restored privy began once the building was dismantled. This process continues today. One item of particular import to the question of construction date was the door locking mechanisms used on the privy doors. As can been seen in photograph 10, the mechanism has a patent date of 1870. According to a professional locksmith, this particular lock was only made for three years, before it was replaced by a different type.[9] Although the patent date is not necessarily the date of the original manufacture and distribution, these facts provide strong evidence for a privy construction date between 1870 and 1873. We also note that the remaining shutter dogs to the privy match those found on the Mansion.

Privy Artifacts. The meager return of artifacts from within the privy vault was the single biggest disappointment of the investigation and can be directly attributable to the shallow design of the vault to enable periodic clean-out. The soil in the vault was of no great age, consisting of six inches of dark brown, loose, and granular loam. The archaeologists did not observe any change in the type or color of the soil the vault.

Each half of the feature fill was excavated in two, three-inch levels down to the brick privy floor; the artifacts recovered are enumerated in Table 1. The only patterning of note within the artifact assemblage is the gender stratification in the artifacts between the two sides. There is no temporal stratification of the artifacts between the two excavation levels and the types of artifacts discarded tend to reflect the dominant role of a sporting club (the RDCC) in the history of the property as a number of items directly reflect sporting or leisure activities. These include a shotgun shell, beer bottle fragments ("medium brown glass"), cigar and cigarette parts, disposable plastic eating utensils, and baseball string. The shotgun shell is marked BLANK on the exterior of the casing; these blanks are used by the RDCC to fire a small signal cannon used in their sailboat races.[10]

Other than a few fragments of transparent bottle glass fragments, there were no artifacts that are so common to privy assemblages, such as ceramic plates, bowls, etc., used to prepare and serve food. There were a few older items within the artifact assemblage, such as a medicine bottle neck and lip and an older-style screw top bottle (possibly for food condiments), but these were not confined exclusively to the lower excavation level and more recent plastic items were also found in the lowest soil deposits.

Photograph 10. Restored door latch and key. Note date stamped on latch.

The Shipman Mansion Privy in Historical Perspective

Investigation of the Shipman Mansion privy revealed various details in its construction that point to a degree of professional design and construction previously unimagined. Most importantly, archaeological evidence in the form of roofing slate shims ties construction of the privy to that of the Shipman Mansion; privy hardware also points to a construction date in the early 1870s. The evident contemporaneity of the two structures is also consistent with the high quality of design and execution in the building of the two structures. However, while the circa 1870 construction date for the Shipman Mansion falls within the period of popularity for the Second Empire style (1865–1900), the design of the privy appears to have been cutting edge if not completely innovative for the United States in the 1870s. The privy exhibits many design characteristics that only became more widely employed as part of the Sanitary Movement in the U.S. at the end of the nineteenth century.

A focused concern on human sanitation as a public health issue first emerged in the 1830s and 1840s in major metropolitan centers found in England, France, and Germany. At the time, a germ-theory for disease did not exist, but no one was oblivious to the connection between filth (of any origin) and disease. Poverty was known to be a third factor in this equation as well. Different vectors were held responsible for disease transmission, perhaps the most popular prior to the twentieth century being the "miasma" or "airs" emanating from sewers, cesspools, swamps, etc. Urban slums were the focus of early sanitation measures as the environments where human overcrowding and abundant sources of miasmatic airs were in greatest proximity and disease most prevalent.

Concern with public sanitation emerged in the northeastern United States shortly after efforts to improve urban conditions in London and elsewhere were made public in the 1830s.[11] However, effective response on the part of public officials to these concerns was retarded until near the end of the nineteenth century. Various reasons for this delay have been cited. Foremost amongst them was the national focus on sectional conflicts revolving around race and slavery, which eventually ruptured into a Civil War. Other social reform movements also absorbed public discourse—notably women's suffrage, prison reform, temperance—and competed with sanitation for the public's attention and energy.[12] Finally, it has been noted that whereas scientific authorities early on recognized the need for *national* measures to diminish disease and promote health, this philosophy ran headlong into the strikingly familiar argument that it impinged on personal freedom.[13] At least into the third quarter of the nineteenth century, these political concerns would trump unified national measures to improve the nation's sanitation and thereby its health.

States did not begin to exercise effective control over public sanitation until the post-bellum period. The New Jersey Sanitary Association was formed in 1874,[14] but the New Jersey State Board of Health was not established until three years later, in 1877 (State of New Jersey Department of State).[15] It was not until the first quarter of the twentieth century that regulations were promulgated by the State Board of Health for the construction of privies and cesspools, such as that for Bayonne (June 20, 1912); Bloomfield (May 26, 1915); Perth Amboy (September 17, 1913); Hackensack (January 7, 1915)—to name a few.[16] Concomitant advice was being provided by sanitary experts on the appropriate design for modern privies, from the then-novel perspective that maintaining public health, rather than privacy, was their primary function:

> In accordance with this widespread conception, the chief idea usually sought is to hide a person momentarily from view, and as a clump of bushes or a grove of trees secures such privacy, many persons avoid the privy and simply use some secluded private spot. This popular conception of an outhouse is reflected not only in the standard, but also in some medical dictionaries. Thus, *Webster's Dictionary* defines a privy as "A necessary house or place; a back-house." ... The modern sanitary idea of the purposes of a privy: To the sanitarian the chief purpose of a privy is to prevent soil pollution, and thereby (by properly collecting the excreta) to prevent the spread of disease. Modesty and privacy are, to the mind of the sanitarian, laudable objects, but infinitely secondary when compared with the great object of saving human life by preventing the spread of disease. As substitute for the dictionary definition of a privy, I would suggest the following: A privy is an outhouse designed, primarily, to prevent soil pollution and hence to prevent the spread of disease through dissemination of disease germs contained in the excreta; secondarily, to insure privacy and safeguard modesty to persons responding to the daily calls of nature.[17]

By the time of the First World War, a variety of different sanitary systems for privies were proposed. Some of the design features that are mirrored in the construction of the Shipman Mansion privy are the following:

> Privy vaults below the surface of the ground should be of masonry, either brick or concrete. The masonry floor must be constructed so as to be water-tight, also be well plastered on the inside to secure a smooth surface which can be readily washed and cleaned. In form, they be rectangular, if built of brick. They may be round or with plane sides having rounded corners, if made of concrete. Every underground vault should have its walls built surrounding ground surface to a height of at least eight inches in order to prevent the entrance of surface water.
>
> In size, underground vaults should be small rather so as to require relatively frequent cleaning. The form and location with respect to the shelter house should allow of cleaning without taking up the floor of the house or, indeed, entering it.[18]

This description of the ideal privy vault is that of the Shipman Mansion's, with the exception that the Mansion's privy is not mortar or concrete lined.

Other recommended sanitary design features include:

> A vent not less than 3 inches in diameter should be carried from the tank through the roof of the privy house, and this vent should be screened to prevent the possibility of flies finding their way down the vent.[19]
>
> The ventilators are very important additions to the privy, as they permit a free circulation of air and thus not only reduce the odor but make the outhouse cooler. These ventilators should be copper-wire-screened in order to keep out flies and other insects. There should be at least 4 (better 5), arranged as follows: One each side of the box; one each side the room near the roof; and a fifth ventilator, over the door, in front, is advisable.[20]

The Skinny on the Privy

And:

> Latticework, flowers, and vines.—At best, the privy is not an attractive addition to the yard. It is possible, however, to reduce its unattractiveness by surrounding it with a latticework on which are trained vines or flowers. This plan, which adds but little to the expense, renders the building much less unsightly and much more private.[21]

As described at the beginning of this report, a novel solution to the problem of proper ventilation of the privy was employed: creating a hollow space between the walls separating the men's and women's side of the privy and a roof cupola that permitted venting through the roof system. No evidence for the use of screening was found during the excavation but if it had in fact been used at some point, installation of screening would have post-dated the circa 1870 construction of the privy. Also mentioned in the site description was the presence of a latticework screen surrounding the two most visible sides of the privy. This was not original to the construction of the privy, but may have replaced an original screening, as recommended by Stiles.

What is remarkable about the Shipman Mansion privy is that it incorporates several design features in privy construction at least two decades before they became the recommended standard in the United States. We know that Paul and Alice Shipman travelled in Europe for two years after their wedding in 1868 and presumably while their mansion in Edgewater Park was under construction.[22] A future avenue of research would be to look for antecedents to the Shipman Mansion privy in Europe, which, as we have noted above, had advanced ahead of the United States in its concern over public sanitation. For example, the illustration of English privy design from 1884 shares several design elements with the Shipman privy (figure 4). Note the double-walled, single vault design, apparently with hollow walls and a cupola roof for venting.

Conclusion

The privy at the Shipman Mansion was fully restored in 2018 and with it an important piece of the mansion's history (photograph 11). We still don't have an adequate explanation for why such an elaborate privy was erected for a middle-aged couple, but now we do know that it was built at the same time as the mansion. Perhaps the Shipmans were more socially active—or anticipated being more socially active when they built the property—than we realize. What we can now appreciate from what we've learned about the design of the privy is that they were progressive thinkers and concerned that even the lowly function of the privy should be provided with the most modern and innovative facility.

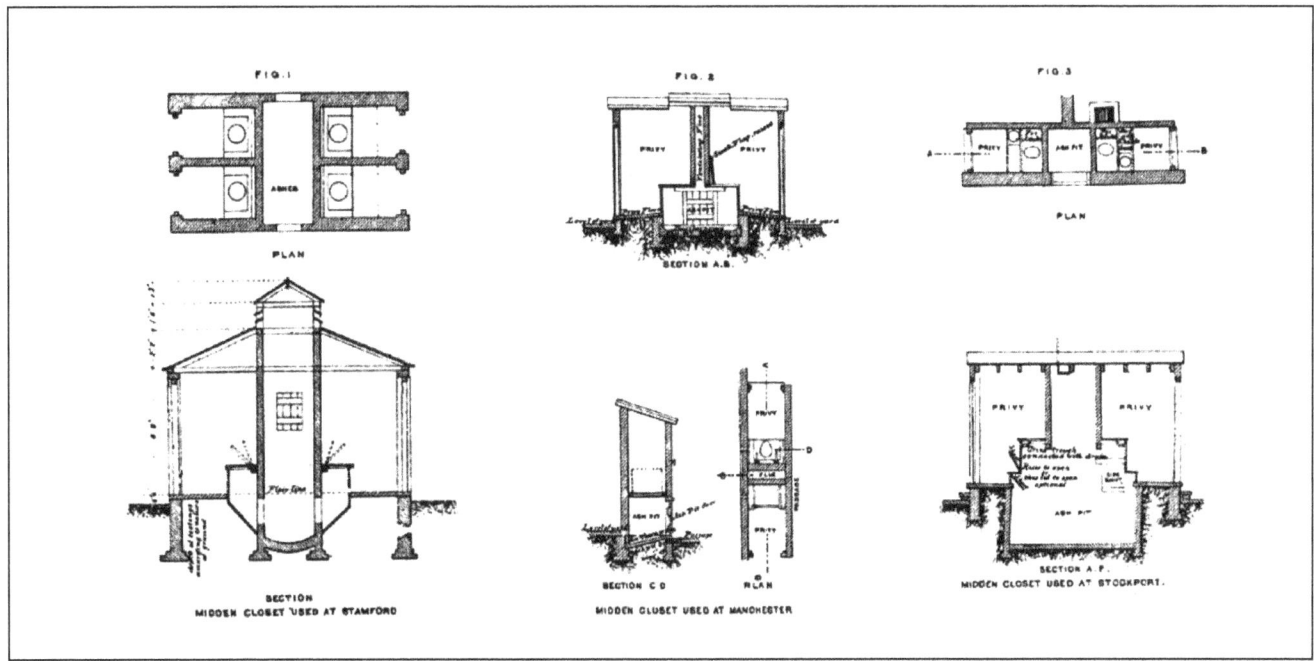

Figure 4. 1884 English privy designs. Image source from www.sewerhistory.org.

Photograph 11. The fully restored privy, looking southwest.

Acknowledgements

The author would like to thank the many members of the SMF, RDCC and NJCT who made this investigation possible. Foremost amongst them is Mrs. Norma Carter, without whose enthusiasm this project would not have been possible and Mr. David Weinberg for his able assistance with the archaeological field investigation. We would also like to thank the entire board of directors of the SMF, Messrs. Donald Wood, Douglas Campbell, Michael Dmochowski, William VanKeuren and Edward Leaf for information they provided to the project team. Our collaboration with Mr. Carl Blaetz of Long Neck Partners, the contractor responsible for the privy restoration, was enjoyable as well as informative; Mr. Blaetz shared several details of the original privy's construction that are included in this report. Finally, we would like to thank Ms. Cathy Goulet of the NJCT for her guidance and compliance review of this project.

About the Author

John Lawrence is a former resident of Burlington City and currently serves as an archaeologist for the Federal Emergency Management Administration. He has practiced archaeological and historical investigations across the mid-Atlantic states over the past thirty years. His professional experience has included original research into the history and prehistory of South Jersey, in which he holds a special interest in historic farmsteads and farm life.

Endnotes

1 Paul Shipman was 42 years old when he married Alice Davidson (age unknown) in 1868. They were a socially prominent couple with wealthy connections, though not within the local Edgewater Park environs. Their wider sphere of influence included Paul Shipman's friendship with Joshua Speed and James W. Hemming, both of Louisville, Kentucky. Both Speed and Hemming had been business associates of Abraham Lincoln during his Springfield, Illinois, days. Alice maintained a friendship with Mary Todd Lincoln. They might have anticipated raising a family, although Alice was reported to be not well physically, with an unnamed malady.

2 "Brilliant Journalist Who Urged Neutrality of Kentucky in Civil War Again Proved Newspaper Fame is Fleeting," *Lexington Herald* (Lexington, KY), Sunday, October 29, 1922, 10.

3 The Shipmans took out a mortgage to purchase the property in 1870, using funds made available by Alice Shipman's father, but had not managed to amortize the mortgage by the time of their passing, 47 years later.

4 Burlington County Deed Book 620:212.

5 Alice's brother, Maj. Henry G. Davidson, served in the

The Skinny on the Privy

Union Army and died near the end of the Civil War; this, however, would have been prior to the Shipman's purchase of the property in Edgewater Park. Alice D. Shipman, "An Illinois Pioneer and His Associates," in *The Phrenological Journal,* vol. 77, no. 3 (1883): 119–127, 127.

6 Now part of the RDCC property; the wharf was constructed sometime in the mid-1850s, probably as part of the planned residential development of what was to become Edgewater Park.

7 Only three bricks were found in the top course at the northwest corner, but it is likely that it originally contained four, as at the other corners.

8 Mr. Carl Blaetz, Personal communication, May 2018.

9 Mr. Don Woods, personal communication, October 2018.

10 Mr. William VanKeuren, personal communication, June 2018.

11 Howard D. Kramer, "History of the Public Health Movement in the United States, 1850 to 1900," PhD thesis, State University of Iowa, 1942, 3.

12 Ibid., 18. John Duffy, *The Sanitarians: A History of American Public Health* (Chicago, IL: University of Illinois Press, 1990), 66–67.

13 Kramer, 113.

14 Ibid. 141.

15 State of New Jersey Department of State, Department of Health. Claude Epstein has written about the development of sanitation laws in New Jersey in "Plagues and Public Policy: How South Jersey Cleaned Up Its Act," *SoJourn*, vol. 2, no. 2 (Winter 2017/18): 69–82.

16 Similar regulations were being enacted in cities across the United States at the same time.

17 Wardell Stiles, "The Sanitary Privy" in *Public Health Reports*, vol. 25, no. 17 (1910): 546.

18 Charles B. Ball, "Privy Vaults. Safe Disposal of Bodily Wastes a Necessity," *Proceedings of the Academy of Political Science in the City of New York*, vol. 2, no. 3 (April 1912): 259–351, 262.

19 Charles T. Nesbitt, "Sewage Disposal under Rural Conditions: Soil Pollution and the Practical Use of the L. R. S. Method for Excreta Disposal in the Country and Suburbs" in *Public Health Reports*, vol. 32, no. 27 (July 1917): 1077.

20 Stiles, 551.

21 Ibid., 551.

22 "Col. Paul R. Shipman Dies at Edgewater Park," *The Evening Public Ledger* (Philadelphia, PA), Wednesday March 21, 1917, 6.

Most people have some familiarity with Atlantic City's segregated Chicken Bone Beach, located at the foot of South Missouri Avenue. It was a rather famous section of sand and surf in America's Playground, but which carried with its designation a malicious tone of racial animus. Today, the history of this beach is celebrated! Other resort cities along the Jersey shore were less restrictive to Blacks relative to beach use. In this view, we see a group of summer revelers enjoying their time in the sun at Ocean City. Pictured here are Mr. & Mrs. Robinson of Jersey City; Mrs. Lee and Miss Edna Murry of Washington, D.C.; Imogen Towns of Philadelphia; Sara J. Wilson and Henry Wilson, both of Norristown, Pennsylvania. Despite the tenor of the times, these people of color could still smile for the camera.

No Wild Rivers in South Jersey

An Evironmental Biography

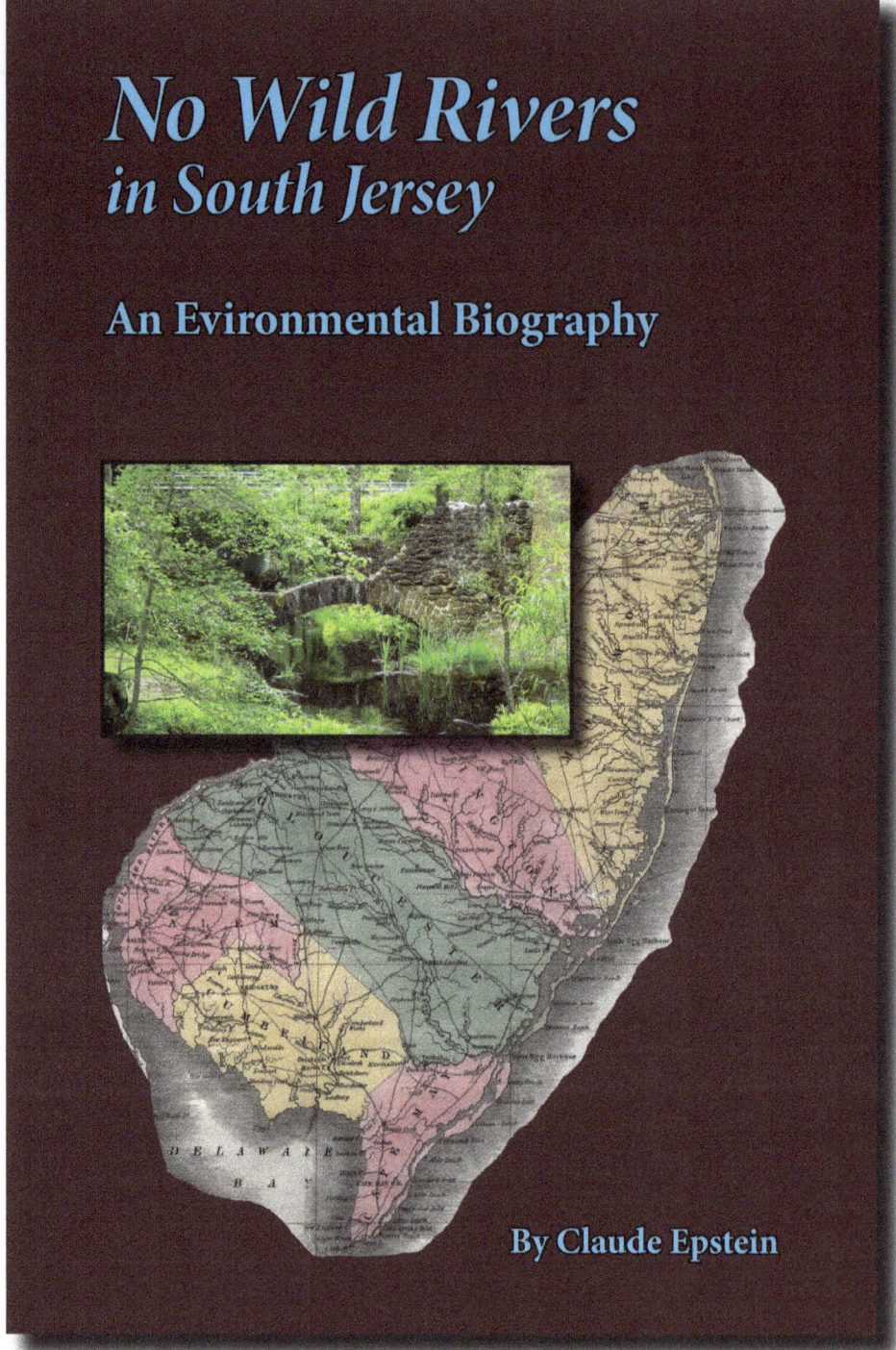

By Claude Epstein

No Wild Rivers in South Jersey. At the printers now! *No Wild Rivers in South Jersey* by Claude Epstein is the first book to impart information on the full impact that cultural adaption of the region's numerous waterways has wrought on the streams and adjacent banks. In the past, books that discussed individual rivers and creeks have been published. Some texts serve as canoe guides, such as James and Margaret Cawley's pioneering work, *Exploring the Little Rivers of New Jersey*, first published in the 1940s. *No Wild Rivers*, however, takes the discussion to a whole new level, covering the indigenous peoples and their stream usage, and then providing coverage of the successive waves of European arrivals, including the Swedes, the Dutch, and the English. As these representatives of Western civilization arrived in South Jersey, each group of settlers began to have serious impacts on the waterways they encountered, establishing landings, wharves, and piers, constructing various types of watermills, rechanneling streams, raising banks to enclose meadows, and digging canals. As the text moves into the nineteenth and twentieth centuries, the author explores the impact of sourced and non-sourced pollutants and runoff and the resultant bank erosion. The author even provides a collection of historical accounts that demonstrate how others down through history viewed South Jersey and its creeks and rivers. The text is engaging and the numerous illustrations and maps augment the author's explanation of why the South Jersey landscape of today contains *No Wild Rivers*.

A publication of the South Jersey Culture & History Center. Hard cover, 453 page. See stockton.edu/sjchc/ for ordering details.

Claude Epstein came to South Jersey in 1971 as one of the founding faculty of Stockton University, where he ultimately became Professor of Environmental Studies. He founded its Environmental Studies Program and assisted in developing other parts of the University. He soon came to appreciate South Jersey's uniqueness—its people, its history, but especially its natural environment. Throughout his forty years at Stockton, he enjoyed teaching his students and took them on many field trips studying the hydrology of the streams in the Pine Barrens. On these trips he recognized how the geologic and land-use history created its current riverscapes. That is what this book is about.

The Artist and the Lighthouse

Text and Illustrations by Hal Taylor

On the sunny shores of the Delaware Bay, at the mouth of the Maurice River, in Maurice River Township, Cumberland County, in the town of Heislerville, New Jersey, sits the East Point Lighthouse. A two-story, whitewashed brick house with a light tower perched atop a bright red roof rising from the marsh, it keeps watch over the broad expanse of the bay.

It is one of the most reproduced images in the state, if not in the country, attracting artists and photographers from near and far. A visit will almost invariably include someone with an easel set up nearby, rendering their artistic interpretation of this idyllic setting with varying degrees of expertise; some with very little, and a few with more perspective than you might imagine.

Built in 1849, it was originally designated the Maurice River Lighthouse but changed to the present name in 1912 to avoid confusion with neighboring navigational aids, the Maurice River Range Lights, erected in 1898. The mouth of the Maurice River was the epicenter of the vast Delaware Bay oyster industry, hosting around 500 working boats during the busy season, making the need for markers abundantly clear.

Over a span of 62 years, ten different keepers lived there and maintained the light, beginning with William W. Yarrington, who stayed on the job only two weeks. He was followed by Francis Elberson, a more permanent replacement, lasting until 1853. The final keeper was Lindwood Spicer, who was let go in 1911 when the beacon became automated. An acetylene light was installed which could stay lit for weeks at a time without refueling. Live-in custodians were still required for general maintenance, but since there was little actual light keeping, the salary dropped from $500 per year to a token $1.

In 1941, the lamp was extinguished due to wartime concerns and stayed dark for thirty-nine years. In 1955, the property was sold to the State of New Jersey which had no interest in the lighthouse itself, only access to the water. The structure was boarded up and abandoned. In 1971, while the Maurice River Historical Society was negotiating with the state to restore the site, vandals broke into the lighthouse and started a fire that destroyed the lantern room, the roof, and a good deal of the interior. Despite the setback, the Society persevered and raised the funds to repair the lantern room and the roof. They also convinced the U.S. Coast Guard to reactivate the lighthouse in 1980, and it still shines brightly today.[1]

After the 1971 fire, it was clear that surveillance was needed so that the same ugly shenanigans were not repeated. The interior of the lighthouse had not yet been repaired, but Maurice River Township donated and moved onto the lighthouse grounds a small, unused cottage to be used by live-in caretakers, free of charge.

In the early 1990s, archivist Joseph Mathews and his wife Roberta Ferro were two of the people chosen for the position and they moved into their new home. Having recently lived in the verdant splendor of Mount Holly in Burlington County, New Jersey, it was shocking for them to suddenly experience the vast openness of the bay shore, unbroken to the horizon, flooded with dazzling brightness. The cottage was cramped but they had only to step outside to experience an entirely different world. Joe was working and staying in Philadelphia three days a week and commuting to East Point for the remainder. He recalls that while traveling back to the lighthouse, "the last few minutes of the drive as I emerged under the trees along East Point Road would usually give me a feeling of openness and release from the shadows."

Although a picturesque setting, it could be lonely at times, so visitors were almost always welcome. Joe vividly remembers one particular visit by members of an artist's cooperative from Chadd's Ford, Pennsylvania, who were looking for interesting settings. Joe and Roberta took them into the lighthouse for a tour, all the way up to the recently repaired lantern room where the light was the strongest. One of the artists, gushing over the views, asked if they could return the following week.

When you think of Chadd's Ford, and are at all familiar with American art, you are likely to think of the Wyeth family. That is where the patriarch of the clan, Newell Convers Wyeth, better known as NC, bought eighteen acres in 1911, after studying with Howard Pyle at his school in Wilmington, Delaware. Pyle is considered the father of American illustration, but NC himself became the premier illustrator of his day, painting ultra-dynamic images for classic literature: *Robin Hood*, *The Last of the Mohicans*, *Treasure Island*, and *Robinson Crusoe*. He was also responsible for two more artists: his son Andrew, and grandson Jamie. But it was Andrew who rose to prominence as arguably the greatest American artist of the twentieth century.[2]

The East Point Lighthouse.

You can imagine Joe's surprise when the group did indeed return the next week with Andrew Wyeth himself, accompanied by his former model Helga Testorf. The two had created quite a stir not only in the art world but in international news when Wyeth released a collection of works that featured images of Helga, many of them nudes, that he had done and kept secret from everyone, including his wife, for years. Both of them were a good bit older now; Helga attended to Andrew as a nurse/caretaker.[3]

At the time of the visit to East Point, Wyeth was in the process of revisiting his heritage. He had been to the Delaware Bay as a boy, with his father and Howard Pyle, on trips to Rehoboth Beach and Cape Henlopen. He was probably not reluctant to visit East Point.

Joe, Roberta, and her friend David once again climbed up to the lantern room, this time accompanied by Andrew and Helga. Joe then had to leave the party and return to his work in Philadelphia. Later, David told Joe that while they were in the lantern room, Wyeth, taken with the vivid lighting, did a quick sketch.

The Artist and the Lighthouse

When David complimented the piece, Wyeth asked him if he would like to keep it. Apparently not realizing who this man was, or the value of what was being offered, David politely refused.

It was not the first time that Wyeth's work had been slighted—even brutalized. In Maine, the Olsen family of "Christina's World" fame, folded up one of his watercolors to patch a broken windowpane. In 1940, one of his first tempera paintings, of his neighbor Adam Johnson's farm at Chadd's Ford, was exhibited at the Carnegie Institute in Pittsburgh. It did not sell, so Wyeth gave it to Johnson. Later when visiting the farmer's home, Wyeth noticed the framed painting hanging in his living room and asked "Isn't it smaller?" Johnson stuttered, "Oh Andy, I . . . I . . . I found a frame over in the dump. Looked so good. So I just sawed it off and it fit fine." Wyeth laughed, "The left side was gone!" Johnson later refused $600 for the amputated painting.[4] During the same period, Andrew painted various scenes at the nearby Koerner farm, most of which he was not pleased with, and left them lying around. Karl Koerner found the discarded paintings and used them to light fires with, or as collateral in poker games.[5]

It seems the vistas from the lantern room of the lighthouse were far better than those at ground level. Trying to enjoy the panorama of the Maurice River Cove, Wyeth found that the beach was piled high with trash bags filled with horseshoe crabs, evidently to be used either for bait or fertilizer. He complained about the obstructions, blocking both the view and the beach, but nothing was done about them. The Chadd's Ford traveling artist's collective then packed up and headed for Cape May.

Things did not improve there, either. Wyeth began another drawing, but while in the process, was approached by a beach tag inspector and told he would either have to buy a beach tag or leave the premises. Disgusted, the company again packed up and left, Wyeth grumbling that one had to pay to do artwork in Cape May! He died in 2009 never having returned to the Jersey Shore.

As for the East Point Lighthouse, it has been fully restored thanks to an $852,000 joint restoration and construction project shared by the Cumberland County Improvement Authority and the Maurice River Historical Society, and funded by the Federal Highway Administration and the New Jersey Historic Trust. The roof was replaced, the exterior bricks were repointed, and the interior was renovated and furnished with tables, chairs, and appointments appropriate to the era, donated by local volunteers and admirers. Heating and air-conditioning were also added. The project was

Andrew Wyeth.

completed under the loving and watchful eye of Nancy Patterson, President and Manager of East Point. Patterson spent her summers sailing and racing small boats in the back bays of nearby Sea Isle City, long before she had ever gazed upon this object of her affection.

The place now looks like a lighthouse keeper is still on the job, but the second oldest lighthouse in the state faces an increasingly urgent issue: erosion. The building sits precariously on the edge of a very hungry Delaware Bay that has been nibbling away at bay shore structures and communities for decades.

And now, in addition to erosion, Patterson and her staff of volunteers are also battling the N.J. Department of Environmental Protection. The State of New Jersey still owns the property, while the DEP oversees leasing, which for the past 50 years has been contracted to the Maurice River Historical Society. That lease expired in March of 2020 and in a move that left Patterson and her staff scratching their heads, the DEP decided not to renew it, explaining they must issue a "request for proposal" to anyone interested in the operation of the lighthouse. No timetable for that process was given, and the lighthouse was closed.

But then, thanks to intervention from local politicians, a temporary lease was negotiated, and it was re-opened in August of 2021.[6]

As of this writing, the lighthouse is protected by only a small barrier of ultimately inefficient geo-tubes, and the DEP is dragging its feet establishing a long-term leasing agreement and arranging for the ultimate physical safety of this historic structure. We can only hope the East Point Lighthouse will survive impending disaster, either natural . . . or man-made.

Acknowledgments

This story comes from Joseph Mathews, Archivist of the Cumberland County Historical Society, and Chairman of the New Sweden Company, Inc. Additional reference material provided by Nancy Patterson, author, illustrator, photographer, and President/Manager of East Point Lighthouse, and Steve Murray, former manager of the Hereford Inlet Lighthouse, board member of the Lighthouse Managers of New Jersey and Historic Cold Spring Village, volunteer consultant to the East Point Lighthouse, author, and playwright.

About the Author

Hal Taylor is an author/artist who has written and illustrated four books that explore various aspects of Delaware Valley History. This article is from his self-published book, *ARTIFACTS: An Illustrated Treasury of Delaware Valley History*. View more of Hal's work at: www.haltaylorillustration.com.

Endnotes

1. *East Point Lighthouse*, http://lighthousefriends.com/light.asp?ID=372.
2. Richard Meryman, *Andrew Wyeth: A Secret Life* (New York: HarperCollins Publishers, Inc., 1996), 29.
3. Meryman, 417.
4. Ibid 190.
5. Ibid 200.
6. Joseph P. Smith, "East Point Lighthouse Issues Spotlighted in N.J. commissioner Bay Shore Tour," *Vineland Daily Journal*, September 1, 2021, https://www.thedailyjournal.com/story/news/2021/09/01/maurice-river-historic-society-license-lease-east-point-lighthouse-dep/5647599001/.

From the *Bridgeton Evening News*, Monday, February 7, 1898, 1.

A North Pearl street lady, who is very fond of her pet cat, was greatly embarrassed last night because of her efforts to please the feline. Early in the evening, bidding her pet an affectionate good night, she went over to her brother's home on Atlantic street for a short call. If there is any one thing that the cat likes it is sweet potatoes. The lady's brother had sweet potatoes "to burn," figuratively, and the lady put several of them in her coat pocket before she left the house.

Then she attended Berean Baptist Temple. When the services were over she, with the rest, arose while the pastor pronounced the benediction. As she did so the sweet potatoes fell noisily to the floor and other worshippers in the near vicinity smiled blandly and smothered a laugh. The lady's face turned crimson, but afterwards she picked up the potatoes—and all for her pet cat.

Jarrad, Last of the Pineys

George Agnew Chamberlain

This short story was first published in The Saturday Evening Post *in 1925. In it, George Agnew Chamberlain (1878–1966) has provided a study of two separate New Jersey existences. It describes the clash between progressive, early twentieth-century society, where one person in four owns a car, truck or tractor, and the last of the Pineys. Despite dissimilar understandings of success, friendship, and life, the two protagonists, so very different, forge a true fellowship.*

* * *

Take a road map of the state of New Jersey, spread it out, flash a glance down its narrow length, and what leaps out to meet the eye? A vast triangle bounded by an encroaching web of red ink. The red ink stands for good roads in five denominations: state highway system—hard surface roads of durable character, improved roads, roads under construction, non-state hard surface roads and improved roads. The white stands for the absence of all or any of these.

Look closely at the blank space, and instead of Sahara desert, read Burlington and Ocean counties. Red along the coast, red South of the broad mark of the White Horse Pike, all red North of a line drawn from Camden through Medford, Browns Mills and Lakehurst to Toms River—and in between, a region so sparsely dotted with names that it might well be labeled quotation mark "unexplored."

Here is the stronghold of the Pineys, trotted out from year to year in the public press as a scarecrow tribe left behind by time. Every once in so often the Pineys have been good for a sensation, traduced by the very circumstance that first gave them news value. As they were to the original Reporter who struck the yellow vein of paydirt, so must they be to the last if he would pad his purse in the front page of the Sunday magazine supplement. Every reader knows the formula—a family of seven in a one room hut; heaps of rags on the clay floor for a common bed; squalor, amorality, incest, idiocy; and finally the deduction of a race of savages, wild men of the woods who live on berries and roots and mouth an unintelligible tongue. Thus it has come to pass that he who ventures to the borders of their fastnesses and airs an inquiring mind is met by a hard stare in a valuable negation:

> "Pineys? What do you mean? Huts? You want to see huts? Well, let me tell you, there are no huts. They live in houses, like you and me, and are just as good as you in me. You're looking for something you won't find, and if you take my advice, you'll go back and get on a good road. It's no place for a car like yours in there; turn twice and you're lost."

There is no telling how many millions of motorists have hurtled along the Shore Road and the White Horse Pike to Atlantic City, but one would count on the fingers of two hands the dozens who have turned off to the left or right to sample the mysteries of Buckingham, Mount Misery, Woodmansie or the head waters of the Wading River and Rancocas Creek. And yet this region is not what it once was. Barnegat has pushed out a red feeler to the West past Cedar Bridge; Mount Holly has thrown out a tendril to Tabernacle, and Hammonton another to Atsion; while from the north, Browns Mills has run a good road due south through the forest to Chatsworth, incongruously famed as the ancestral estate of the Marquise de Tallyrand-Périgord and of her sister, the Dowager Princess Pogio-Susa Ruspoli. Thus far have great names wandered to rub noses with the despised Pineys.

Even so, he who is not faint of heart, who fears neither solitude nor rutted sandy trails as twisted as the track of a snake, can lose himself in a maze of byways remarkable for their number and interminable monotony. Sand, scrub oak and pine; pine, scrub oak and sand. Miles and miles without seeing a human being or a house.

But though they are so widely spaced, the houses are there; some of them hidden, others looming suddenly in a clearing cluttered with barns, sheds, flowers and an astonishing growth of vegetables. Enter one of them, study it, and you may discover, imbedded amid its rooms and covered on the outside with sheathing, the original one-room log cabin which brought the forgotten Pineys into lurid fame.

Legend once had its basis in fact, but these people have come up. In spite of a vacant face here and there, always ready to break into a smile of peculiar sweetness; in spite of an occasional malformation due to inbreeding, they have been dragged out of the pit of oblivion by three commodities and an influence. Cranberries, swamp Moss and blueberries, demanded in ever increasing quantities by an encroaching outside world, have given the Piney a possible wage of $10 a day for five months in the year, and a mission, run by two ladies in a flivver, has taught him what to do with his money.

However, there remain even today regions in the forest which the most industrious flivver cannot penetrate, and in one of these dwelt the last of the old style Pineys. His name was Jarrad, and because he had once been misunderstood when he tried to say "Jarrad only" in an answer to a question as to the rest of it, he was entered on the books of the crossroads store at Two Heads as Jarrad Ohne, and from that day was so known to the few people with whom he came in contact.

No one, least of all Jarrad, new his exact age. At the time of the close of this story he was probably between thirty-five and forty years old; but there is a mere guess, confused by the fact that while his wiry body seemed withered, his brown eyes held an ingenuous eagerness, a glistening fire, which one ascribes only to extreme youth. These eyes gave the impression of being very much alive and yet imprisoned, as if they were forever trying to leap out and run around and be petted, but were hopelessly anchored to something dull and heavy in the back of his head.

Jarrad could not remember his mother's teaching him the rudiments of reading and writing, but he could recall her burial. To him it was the first of the three high lights of his life. His father had been a morose man, one who walked alone, within his own shadow. When his wife died he had called for no aid from distant neighbors. With hoe, shovel and axe, he had dug a grave at the edge of the swamp back of the cabin, fitted into the hole a rude box made of cedar slabs and laid away within it the body of his wife. Several years later the boy had been faced with the necessity of doing as much and no more for his father. Strangely enough this task, which had called for the utmost exertion of his immature strength as well as of all other faculties, had established no sign post in memory. It was a mere repetition of the first conscious formula of life.

Dating from that event, Jarrad lived alone for many years. On the sunny days of spring he gathered swamp moss, valuable to florists and packers of fine crockery, laid it out to dry; and when he had accumulated the equivalent of a bail, hitched up the mule that lived contentedly on hay in a lean to at one end of the cabin, and drove to the crossroads at Two Heads. It was an all-day trip; but it never seemed long, because there was always the chance that he might meet somebody around anyone of the myriad twistings of the rutted trail. Such wordless encounters within the woods were rare—perhaps one in a month, certainly not more than fifteen in a whole year—but each one of them lighted up a smile and Jarrad's eyes which, like the glow of a northern twilight, lived for a surprisingly long time.

In summer he gathered blueberries literally by the bushel. His father's knocker, scoop and strainer had hung discarded ever since Jarrad learned that the hand-picked berries fetched a better price than knocked ones. Of course, knocking was easier. To place the scoop, hit the bush an expert wack or two, sieve out the green or undersized berries and dump the remainder into the bucket was quick work. But there always remained enough twigs or bits of leaves to betray the process. Besides, none knew better than he where to find the swamp shrubs which yielded the largest and bluest fruit. It was a joy to fill his pail with big berries all of one color—a blue as pale, deep and soft as the edge of the evening sky.

September ushered in cranberry time. Nobody could lawfully forbid the gathering of blueberries on unfenced land; but with cranberries it was different—all the bogs of any size were owned and guarded. Here again Jarrad's minute knowledge of the woods and of every hidden bottom from the headwaters of Cedar Creek to the gurgling course of the Penny Pot stood him in good stead. He knew of strayed bushes in forgotten mudholes far withdrawn from the ken of their rightful owners.

The grocer at Two Heads was a kindly man, but not above trying to find out the secret of the Ohne boy's increasing wealth. He asked questions as to the source of the cranberries, and when Jarrad, smiling with delight at being noticed, impulsively pointed north, south and east, the grocer decided his strange customer was not so simple as he looked and started the legend of Ohne's shrewdness. It was a legend that grew apace among the habitués of the corner store, for while Jarrad's friendly glances were ever eager and open, his tongue was as consistently tied. It occurred to no one that the few words he uttered formed his entire working vocabulary, for there were many he could read and yet never dared tried to pronounce.

The second high light in Jarrad's existence was a veritable blaze, which all but blinded him; in truth, it belonged not so much to his insignificant body as to his exaggerated hunger for companionship as an abstract. No man could see or know the forest more clearly than he, but in all matters not pertaining to the actual physical contact of the woods he lived in an impenetrable fog. To him, formal funerals, marriages, christenings, were almost in the nature of bodiless ideas, interesting in the same way as are the peasant customs of the Bretons to a schoolma'am going abroad.

Into this fog walked a girl—a woman, really, for she was older than he. Anyone else would have been frightened at her appearance—tangled hair, sallow face, with eyes unequally placed, a Mother Hubbard belted above the hips, thus shortened to display several inches of grimy bare legs and grimier feet. But any other woman under the sun would have frightened Jarrad: not this one, for she melted into the background of just the things he had known all his days. It was her presence, disassociated from her misshapen body and her vacant face, that formed a miracle.

While he was absorbed in picking berries from a high bush she had come to stand on its farther side, and presently began silently adding her labor to his, pouring

handfuls of pale-blue fruit into his bucket. It was a day of terrific heat, made resonant by a myriad insect noises. Close to the earth, under the blanket of the shrill din, there was silence. Jarrad was the first to break it, rebuking the girl sharply for including too many undersized berries. She docilely accepted the reproof and corrected her error. They had gone on from bush to bush, and just as naturally they came to his cabin together.

She stayed with him for a year and two months. That was the dream period, the unalloyed idyl, of a meager life. Out of material so crude as to be repulsive to others, Jarrad molded the perfect sphere of happiness. He drank from a brimming cup of content and lived in a state of mild inebriation—a sort of simmering ecstasy. For once, intuition made him genuinely secretive; he had said nothing of the bewildering whirl of the wheel of fortune on his visits to Two Heads.

One day, returning hastily from the grocers, caring little whether any of the innumerable twists in the road should yield a chance encounter or not, he came to the entrance of his cabin and noticed wheel tracks which were not his own. They entered by one side of the grass grown fork and left by the other; but at this stem over the Y there were signs, easily readable, that a horse had stood there for some time, stamping his feet in the sand, apparently hard and dry on the surface, treacherously soft and moist beneath. The woman was gone.

No idea of pursuit occurred to Jarrad; as she had come of her own free will, so she had disappeared. Whether she had been enticed by a chance visitor or coerced by someone with authority over her was an event equally beyond the range of his speculation. She had not seemed beautiful to him at any time nor had he loved her in the sense of devotion to an individual as such; but she had been with him within the fog, and as long as she had stayed and miserable as was her person, from her presence had emanated the warmth and illumination of fellowship. That seemed to him a great thing. To look back upon the months she had spent in his hovel would always be like coming suddenly from the shadow depths of the woods into the sun-lit blaze of a clearing.

At her going he felt a dumb pain to which he could give no name. For a time it even dulled his eyes; but as days lengthened into months it passed, leaving him just as he had been before her advent, only enriched by a knowledge of the possession of buried gold—something he could drag out and gloat over in the lonely hours of the long nights of winter. What mattered now, as before, was not herself, but the sheer miracle of her having been with him.

After four years, which were as like to the four which had preceded her coming as peas from the same pod, we come to the third high light in Jarrad's life. It was concerned with a double murder. Two men in the front seat of a motor car had been shot in the back while driving on one of the many lonely trails that led eventually to Chatsworth. It was evident that whoever committed the outrage had subsequently thrown the gears into reverse, gained momentum, swerved the car sharply and backed it into the brush as deep as it would go. The rear wheels had churned themselves in to the hubs. If the intent had been either to bury the car from sight or to turn it and flee, the purpose had been frustrated by the treacherous sand.

Jarrad happened to drive by the scene of the murder before anyone else. His first impulse after stopping his mule was to leap out and run to the assistance of the car in trouble, but something startlingly grotesque in the pose of its occupants arrested him. Like most woodsmen, however deliberate, he was keen of eye and rapid in deduction. Before he had time to think he knew the two men were dead. He stood up, then climbed on the board seat in his ramshackle wagon, and remained erect for a long time, reading as from an open book.

Here was a language he could understand and for which his mental vocabulary was more complete than that of any other man within a hundred miles. He was even unconscious of effort as he interpreted sign after sign in the exact sequence of the event. It was a vicious story, beginning with the double whang of a revolver and ending with the roar of an impotent engine, quickly stilled because of its terrifying threat of betrayal.

Jarrad had never killed anything in his whole life; he had never trapped a muskrat or skinned a skunk for easy money, even when his exchequer was at its lowest ebb. As for shooting a squirrel when he himself happened to be hungry, he would far rather have starved to death. He could not have explained this uncompromising aversion to slaughter; but it was simple enough, as are all things fundamental. Since the day of his first memory the live things of the woods had been his friends, blood brothers in his solitude. Without knowing it he looked upon their friendship as a recompense for his lack of human companionship. The killing of the least of them was consequently something he could not bring himself to do. Others might, but he would not.

Imagine the effect on such a person of the willful murder of two fellow beings. The world was a lonely

H. J. Mowatt drew both illustrations, which were included in the original printing.

place, and yet someone had not hesitated to do away with two men, possibly two friends. His eyes grew large and his swarthy cheeks were set afire by a glow from the smoldering excitement within him. He was frightened. He did not, however, place the horror on the crime, but on the waste.

"Police," "sheriff," "justice of the peace," were terms which meant nothing to him; hence he omitted the formality of hurrying to report his discovery to the proper authority. Instead, he drove on home at top speed, unharnessed the mule and turned her loose. He scarcely slept that night, and on the next day and the next he stayed within the cabin, held indoors by an instinctive impulse to hide, combined with a strange feeling of shame.

On the third day a posse followed the wagon tracks to his door and arrested him. The county had latterly been much in the public eye by reason of certain atrocious crimes which had remained unraveled and unpunished. The mood of the prosecutor, constables and jury was one which demanded summary action of some sort, even as a measure of self-preservation in the esteem of the community. Consequently, for lack of any better clew, Jarrad was in due course indicted for murder. Upon his appearance in court, the judge, after a single glance, appointed a young lawyer to defend him.

This latest scion of the county bar was a shrewd, somewhat ironical young man who labored under the name of Leonidas Smith, and realized his handicap. Something out of the ordinary, some unusually striking trick of procedure, is necessary to lift a Smith so high above the countless fellow Smiths that his name will stand out alone and be remembered when the smaller plums of the professional legal pie are being handed around. In Jarrad, Mr. Smith had reason to believe he had stumbled on his chance.

Never had a lawyer a more mystifying client, for Jarrad, dragged into close contact with his fellow beings, was a happier man than he had been at any time save for those months set aside from life by companionship with the woman who had come and gone. His body might wince, shrinking from truths, suspicions and accusations which plunged like long-handled spears into the foggy regions of his brain; but his brown eyes never wavered from their proclamation of content, of well-being and such a joy as was quite foreign to Mr. Smith's limited experience.

Here was a man who had lived all his life in a poverty far more abject than the mere lack of riches; who scarcely knew how to read and write; who had no friend to say a good word for him except the storekeeper at Two Heads; who was accused of an atrocious murder; whose body was miserable and raggedly clothed—and who yet carried in his confiding eyes such a look of happiness as Mr. Smith had never before seen.

Idiocy, perhaps. He had heard of those Pineys. Probably the man was guilty; if so, here was the old defense of insanity more than half ready to hand.

But because insanity was so old and worn in a subterfuge, Mr. Smith preferred to have none of it. He wanted something new, something striking, and began an intensive study of Jarrad as a possible forcing bed for an original idea as grotesque as Jarrad himself. He talked to him by the hour and gradually pieced out a fairly true picture of his life. He had approached these conversations in a spirit of good-humored condescension; but without knowing quite when it happened, he awoke suddenly to the fact that he was dealing with a personality so fresh and unused to contact that to touch it anywhere was to light a warm spark.

From that moment Mr. Smith's attitude toward the case and his client changed completely. He was no longer intent on throwing the limelight on his own name and granting to the accused only such benefit as might chance to further his cause. What had begun to matter now was Jarrad himself—Jarrad, as a manifestation of simplicity and of unqualified trust. You couldn't abandon a man who looked at you like that, no matter what he had done. You couldn't turn your back on anyone so utterly confiding as to brush away the hair line between fortitude and faith and make you wonder whether he was the embodiment of courage or merely the reincarnation of God's fool.

In his gropings through Jarrad's past, Mr. Smith inevitably unearthed three events which were like spurs to the imagination. Posthumously, he became an eyewitness to the burial of Jarrad's mother. Against the somber background of scrub oak, pine and bog, he saw the picture as Jarrad himself could not see it—the gaunt body, laid away without a shroud; the glowering man, putting aside pick, shovel and axe to stand thenceforth alone with his thoughts; and finally the little boy, all eyes and tangled hair, rubbing one barefoot against the calf of his other leg as he balanced in uncertain wonder at the edge of the black grave.

When the incident of the visiting woman was revealed in sparse outline, Mr. Smith asked a casual question:

"What was her name, Jarrad?"

Jarrad frowned in concentration before he answered, "I never asked her no name."

"What?" cried Mr. Smith, glad of a chance to smile. "You lived with a woman for more than a year and never found out her name?"

"She never asked mine neither," said Jarrad, his face crinkling into companionable laughter while his eyes remained puzzled.

Then a strange thing happened to his face—it turned grave and sweet in its subconscious allegiance to memory. It was as though a straying breath of air, laden with a faint fragrance of balsam, had slipped through the narrow window to fan his nostrils. They distended; for a moment he was far away from bars and walls, and even from his new-found friend. Forgotten was everything that had come in between; gone the level years of lonely toil, and even the day of horror which had thrown him out of the Pineys into the midst of men. He was back at that instant in life when he had discovered the woman, standing beside him, picking pale-blue berries from the same bush, dropping them into his bucket.

What a day that had been! Hot—so hot that the leaves of towering fox grapes had gasped and turned up the white bellies of their undersides in surrender to the sun. He could still see that startling sheen of silver against the shadowed background of the singing woods. Yes, the woods sang on a day like that—a high, shrill note with a smell to it, vibrating minutely in unison with the dry, sawing wings of a million noisy insects—fanning themselves, talking to one another, all yelling the same thing: "Heat! Heat! Heat!"

"It was a vurry hot day when she come," he murmured, staring absently before him; "and when she go, I feel cold for a long time."

It was Mr. Smith's turn to frown. There were people who could live like that, for weeks, for months, for more than a year, so close to the ground that names did not matter—and Jarrad was one of them. What had they said to each other in all that time? Short phrases must have done the work of whole arguments: "Fetch water." "Get wood." "Where we going?" "Moss." "Blueberries." "Cranberries." "Snowing." "Make the fire." "Two Heads." "You back by night time?" "Ye-ah." A score of words, occasionally changing the order of their march, might have stretched from one end to the other of the happiest year of Jarrad's life.

After a long silence Mr. Smith put another question. "Now what about the murder?" He asked quietly.

"Heh?"

"The murder," repeated Mr. Smith. "You know—the two men dead in the automobile."

"Ah!"

A film seemed to spread over Jarrad's eager face. Smith could see that here was a subject he could not talk about without genuine pain—not the pain of a physical injury, but that deeper agony of the bruised stalk of one's inner self. He gulped and turned red. He displayed all those symptoms of hesitancy, embarrassment and confusion which juries have been wont to accept only too often as presumptive evidences of guilt.

"Go on," prompted Mr. Smith. "Don't be afraid. Tell me about it exactly as it happened."

Jarrad was sitting on a bench set against the wall of his cell. Through the small barred window on his left poured a shaft of light which struck across his face, throwing the web of fine lines upon it into startling relief. He sat with his legs open, his hands placed on his knees and his head fallen forward. Presently he sighed profoundly, slowly raised his head, fixed his eyes on a picture far outside the prison walls and began to talk. In language as lean and direct as an arrow, he told the story of his discovery of the murdered men.

Mr. Smith was surprised and then stupefied by its effect on himself. A strange thing had happened. He was left without a single doubt as to Jarrad's innocence, and also without a single hook upon which he could hang a plausible defense. It had taken him many days to begin to understand Jarrad; how could he expect a dozen men, hard pressed by mob opinion in the lash of a smarting prosecutor's tongue, to learn in a few hours to accept what fell from an apparent half-wit's mouth as the distillation of truth, incapable of distention or adornment?

In desperation, he began to ask a string of questions, all based on motive, which he knew Jarrad could not answer. Why had he not gone for the police, or to his friend, the grocer at Two Heads? Why had he driven his mule at a gallop? Why had he gone home? And, once there, why had he locked himself in for two days? With exasperation, the young lawyer realized that he himself knew the answer to all these questions, but could not make it intelligible in words, and that Jarrad neither knew his motive nor had the capacity to make it evident.

But all these considerations suddenly shriveled into insignificance in the face of Mr. Smith's next astonishing discovery. He had not seen it coming. It had crept upon him slowly from behind, leapt upon his back and struck a penetrating claw into his brain before he knew it was there. Even so, the discovery remained for a moment unbelievable, for who could credit what Mr. Smith now new—that Jarrad had not an inkling of the fact that he was on trial for what was already come to be called the Piney murders?

Mr. Smith left the cell hurriedly and went for a long walk. Here was such a situation as had surely never before confronted a lawyer—an exception to the father of all rules which declares that there is nothing new under the sun. He might, of course, hammer into Jarrad's restricted consciousness the intelligence of his predicament, but that was the last thing he wished to do. Of what would it avail to see a spirit suddenly wither at its innermost source? Any one of us can kill the thing that matters most in another, but to few is it given to keep that thing alive.

From that hour the defense of Jarrad's neck became a merely contributory action. Only if he could conduct this trial in such a way that his friend and client might never know of the horrible accusation against him could Mr. Smith feel that he had risen to the measure of his opportunity. A few days ago he would have looked upon such an attempt as an aberration of his legal mind; but now that he had perceived Jarrad's innocence as something miraculously warm and alive, protected by a thick wall of silence built of unintelligible words, the feat seemed well within the limits of possibility. All that was needed was a summary acquittal.

As he walked rapidly along a wood path, eyes on the ground, hands clenching and unclenching, Mr. Smith wondered if more seasoned lawyers ever felt what he was feeling—a personal and vindictive reaction against a hypothetical miscarriage of justice. He could even imagine himself leaping at the throats of the men who should convict Jarrad of murder. Yes; if they should do that, it wouldn't be safe for him to have a gun in his pocket!

What made things worse was that such a conviction was by no means improbable, owing to the accumulation of onus on the state. The series of atrocious murders, unsolved and unpunished, had made a futility of judges and juries and a laughingstock of detectors of crime, professional and amateur. Great names had faded away in the blight of failure, and even the public at large had come to feel itself duped—a condition which any beginner in the study of mob psychology could size up as loaded with menace to the ancient tradition of the benefit of the doubt.

The times were peculiarly ripe for convictions on circumstantial evidence; and not more than a week before, Mr. Smith had heard two legal lights agree that a certain man, serving a sentence of twenty years in the penitentiary, had been guilty of nothing but fright. Well, if that was a crime, Jarrad was guilty too—even though what he had felt had not been fright, but a horror indistinguishable from fear.

Then, with an abruptness which would have been comical in any onlooker, Mr. Smith's walk came to an end. He stopped with a jolt and stood quite still for the space of thirty seconds, while his eyes brightened, his lips curved into a smile and his head drew slowly erect. After that he turned and sauntered homeward. During the days which followed he saw a great deal of Jarrad, but never again mentioned the murder. He did not consider the time he spent at the jail wasted, for in reading his strange client he was studying the only book of precedents applicable to his cause.

At last the case came to trial and Mr. Smith welcomed the event. He had his defense ready—so ready that he could think of it with a chuckle and dismiss it with a shrug. His smiling confidence created something of a stir, but its effect was as nothing compared with that of the prisoner's bearing. It amused Mr. Smith to watch the puzzled expression on the faces of the judge, of the jurors and, most of all, of the audience, for he knew what it was that puzzled them. They were stumped by the fact that when they looked at Jarrad Ohne they saw a prisoner in the dock; but when Jarrad's eyes chanced to look at them they caught their breath, overwhelmed by a visualization of release. It was as if the abstract idea of freedom could be reduced to something more substantial than an essence—something as real as a friendly dog, roaming around the room, wagging his tail, asking to be petted by every stranger's hand.

But when the prosecuting attorney began to pile up his circumstantial evidence, it was Mr. Smith's turn to wonder if he was dreaming. The confidence he had in his argument for acquittal almost deserted him. He was appalled at the manner in which details, casual and trifling in themselves, could be linked together by a mind with a fixed goal in view so that they seemed to form an unbreakable chain, a web without a loophole. He realized what no amount of reading and didactic warning had been able to drill into his head—the abysmal treachery of indirect evidence. But in the end he regained his assurance.

"Your Honor," he began, "one point stands out above all others in the able presentation made by the state, and that is the clearness with which it has been established that the perpetrator of this outrage was cold-blooded enough to sit on the knees of the dead driver and back the car of his victims off the road into the scrub growth, almost but not quite out of sight of passers-by.

"My insignificance as a lawyer is emphasized by the fact that I have been appointed to defend a man so destitute of money, friends and reputation that no other voice has been raised in protest against his indictment. But I wish the court and the prosecution to know that if I believed the defendant to be guilty of this atrocious murder I would immediately withdraw and let justice take its course rather than traffic for specious fame with the safety of the community."

The judge bowed solemnly in recognition of the noble sentiments of the youthful defending attorney; the prosecutor smiled cynically; the jury and many of the spectators stared unbelievingly. Only Jarrad, tremendously impressed at the ready flow of long and meaningless words, gasped with admiration, nodded encouragingly and grinned from ear to ear. He was delighted that he and his friend should simultaneously appear thus prominently in the public eye.

"Your honor," continued Mr. Smith, "before any witnesses are called, and especially before the defendant is sworn, I wish to present an exhibit too large to be introduced into this building. I believe it will have a decided influence on the course of this case. I consequently take the liberty to beg that court be adjourned to the yard for a few minutes."

The judge conceded the request. The prisoner, under escort, was led out first; the judge followed, and in his train went clerk, counsel and spectators. Court was called to order in the shade of the jail wall where a few privileged cars were parked. Mr. Smith walked around one of them, took up an easy position with his foot on the running board, and leaned inward, resting one elbow on the back of the front seat.

"Come here, Jarrad."

Jarrad glanced around questioningly. His face was solemn, but not perturbed; it had the intent, earnest look of a child learning a new game. The judge nodded; the constable gave him a push forward. He went to join his counsel at the farther side of the car and thus was placed facing the assembly of authorities and on lookers. Mr. Smith laid his hand on the wheel.

"Jarrad," he asked, "what is this?"

"Automobile," said Jarrad eagerly.

"And this?" asked Mr. Smith, switching on the light, which threw pale moons on the red brick wall.

"Automobile," answered Jarrad.

"And this?" continued Mr. Smith as he leaned over and pressed the starter till it ground like a broken coffee mill.

"Automobile," declared Jarrad fervently.

"Now, Jarrad, come here." Mr. Smith led the way to the back of the car, knelt down and turned the cock of the gas tank. "What's that?" he asked as the gasoline began to trickle.

"Water," said Jarrad.

"No, no!" cried Mr. Smith. "Don't be stupid. Take your time and think. Don't say another word until I tell you to speak. Kneel down."

Jarrad obeyed, his mind more than acquiescent, but his body wary against his will by force of its long training in caution. Mr. Smith cupped one hand and caught some of the gasoline.

"So. Don't be afraid. Catch some of it in your hand like this."

Jarrad held out a browned and grimy paw. The gasoline had a warm, soft feeling. Its exhalation made it seem to creep actively. His hand quivered.

"Now don't say anything yet. Just smell it—taste it, if you like—it won't hurt you. Here, watch this."

With his free hand Mr. Smith drew out a handkerchief, sopped it in the gas, turned off the flow, tossed the handkerchief to a safe distance, went to it, struck a match and set it afire.

Jarrad, Last of the Pineys

As it blazed he drew erect.

"Is that water?" he cried. "You know it isn't! Would water burn like that? Now tell a judge what it is."

"Automobile," declared Jarrad vehemently.

There was a long pause. Mr. Smith dusted off his knees, then threw up his head and faced the judge.

"Your Honor," he said gravely, "we live in a community where one person in every four owns a motor car, a tractor or a truck. It has become natural to us—judge, jurors and lawyers alike—to presuppose a certain knowledge of mechanics in every grown man. That fact comprises the only vestige of excuse for the stupidity with which the accused has been arraigned, indicted and prosecuted for a crime for which you or I or any man or boy present might have been tried with as much more reason. I move the case be dismissed."

"Motion granted," said the judge, a congratulatory twinkle in his eye. "Prisoner discharged."

"You are free, Jarrad," said his young counsel.

Jarrad was still on his knees. He looked up at Mr. Smith, at the judge and his aids, who were already hurrying away, and at the curious crowd, studying him with the rapt faces of children at the Zoo.

"Free?"

"Just that and no more. The law provides conveyance for suspected persons and convicts, but none for a man who has done no wrong. I'm afraid you'll have to walk, but you are free to go back home."

"Home, eh?" asked Jarrad, frowning.

"Yes; to the Pineys."

Jarrad had enough money in the lining of his boot to have paid his defender quite a respectable fee, and much more than enough to provide himself with any grade of transportation; but no one present, not even Mr. Smith, had sufficient imagination to overcome the deduction that cash and such tattered clothing must be strangers to each other. Much less was there anyone in the curious group who could sense that for one more hour of sociable imprisonment Jarrad would gladly have handed over his entire savings.

He saw his lawyer turn from him with a friendly nod and the throng begin to melt. The eager light went out of his eyes. He got to his feet, raised his head, glanced at the sun, pointed his nose like a hound taking a scent and started off in a beeline for the Pineys. At the first corner, however, he turned back and intercepted Mr. Smith on his way into the courthouse.

"Say," he asked with an uncertain smile, "are me and you friends?"

"You bet we are," replied Mr. Smith, holding out his hand. "Don't you ever dare come into town without looking me up. Do you understand that, Jarrad?"

"Sure!" cried Jarrad, laughter suddenly reborn in his eyes. "It's a long way to my place. I buy me an automobile tomorrow—come to town every Saturday."

The judge was waiting on the courthouse steps to speak to Mr. Smith.

"That was a queer client I handed you," he said, "but I offer you my hearty congratulations. I'll never forget the way you handled the case. I'm afraid there was no fee, but you needn't mind that."

"Judge," said Mrs. Smith, "you are patting me on the back for having won one case, while I'm congratulating myself on having won quite another."

"What do you mean by that, young man?" asked the judge with a puzzled frown.

"Well, for one thing, my client isn't a pauper by a long shot. He's going to buy himself a motor car tomorrow."

"So he paid you, did he?"

"No, he didn't—not in cash. He would have if I had asked him, but I couldn't."

"Why not?"

"Because if I had I'd have lost the main case I won for him."

"That's enough of riddles. Speak out or I'll begin to think your head is turned."

"Not mine, judge," said Mr. Smith with a confident smile. "Think this over: Your Honor has just presided at a murder trial where the prisoner didn't know he was accused of murder, doesn't know it yet, and never will know it if you and I can keep our mouths shut."

First published, "Jarrad, Last of the Pineys," *The Saturday Evening Post*, 197, no. 48 (May 30, 1925): 5, 113–21.

George E. Weber:
Burlington County's Greatest Athlete

Dennis McDonald

A case could be made that Star Bicyclist George E. Weber, who rode in the 1880s, was one of the greatest athletes to come out of Burlington County, New Jersey. That is heady company considering the county is home to Carl Lewis, Carli Lloyd, and Franco Harris.

Weber was born in Burlington on May 18, 1866.[1] In 1884, upon reaching the age of seventeen, he moved to Smithville, where he obtained employment at the H. B. Smith Machine Company as an apprentice machinist.[2] The company had recently begun manufacturing the Star Bicycle. Already proficient in riding the Star,[3] Weber took advantage of the half-price bicycles that the company offered to its employees and the recently opened eleventh-of-a-mile oval track built for the company workers.[4]

How did a company that manufactured woodworking machinery get involved in the cycling craze that was sweeping the country? In 1880, Hammonton, New Jersey, inventor George Washington Pressey had recently patented two designs (#233,640 and #234,722) for a velocipede[5] (a lightweight rider propelled wheeled vehicle).[6] His patents had gotten around those patents that the Pope Manufacturing Company held, producers of the Columbia high wheel bicycle, the most popular bicycle of the time. Although Pressey had designed and built two or three of the high wheel bicycles in his blacksmith shop,[7] he was not equipped to manufacture hundreds of bicycles. After lengthy negotiations, he signed an agreement with company owner Hezekiah Bradley Smith in January 1881.[8] The H. B. Smith Machine Company would now manufacture his Star Bicycle.

When George Weber arrived at Smithville, the H. B. Smith Machine Company had a stable of racers that competed throughout the East Coast and riders that gave exhibitions with the Star Bicycle. They included Charles Frazier, Thomas Finley, Joseph Powell, Edward Burns and Charles Chickering. Weber quickly made a name for himself the first year he was with the company. He made his debut on the track at the Capital Club Races held at Washington (D.C.)[9] in May 1884. He won the one-mile race for novices in three minutes and 25 seconds while racing for the Star Club of Smithville, New Jersey.[10] He also finished

George E. Weber poses with his nickel-plated American Star Bicycle in a studio portrait. Weber was one of the most famous cyclists in the world in 1885 and 1886. Photograph Courtesy of the Burlington County Board of Commissioners/Division of Parks.

George E. Weber stands for a studio portrait in his riding suit with some of his medals pinned to his chest. Photograph Courtesy of Janice Weber Hoffman.

second in the three-mile open handicap race. In June, he raced in a two-mile amateur bicycle race at Jumbo Park in a Philadelphia, Pennsylvania, tournament where he finished first in a field of seventeen competitors.[11]

Weber continued training in Smithville for the biggest bicycling meet of the year, held every September in Springfield, Massachusetts. He went to the meet with a small group of riders and a trainer. Weber set a new American record for three miles in eight minutes, 50¾ seconds.[12]

The biggest ride of Weber's young career did not occur on a track. In October of 1884, he entered the Boston Bicycle Club's 100-Mile Road Race. Ten riders started the competition at 6:30 a.m. at Harvard Square in Boston. George E. Weber finished in nine hours and twenty minutes, beating the previous record by 27 minutes. While others stopped for lunch, Weber did not for fear of upsetting his stomach.[13]

1885 was an even bigger year for Weber. He won three races in Philadelphia in April and two in St. Louis in May. Next, he went to New Haven, Connecticut, and won the Twenty-Five Mile League of American Wheelman (L.A.W.) Championship in one hour, four and four-fifths seconds (a new record). In July, he was first in Springfield, Ohio; he won the half-mile L.A.W. Championship and a ten-mile race. Later that month, he went to Chicago, Illinois, where he won the Fifteen-Mile League of American Wheelmen (L.A.W.) Championship and a one-mile race.

He went to Springfield, Massachusetts, for the biggest meet of the year as the man to beat. Weber won the one-and-one-half-mile race, the three-mile race, and the four-mile race. During the ten-mile race, it was suggested that the racers continue to see how far they could go in an hour. Weber finished second to a British cyclist at ten miles, but the top three riders continued on, and each set new records: Weber with an American record of twenty miles, 290 yards in an hour.[14]

In October, Weber traveled to Boston to defend his crown in the Third Annual 100-Mile Road Race. He more than defended his title. He set a new American Record, finishing in six hours and 57 minutes, cutting more than two hours off his 1884 record.[15] The road race captivated Americans. *The Boston Globe* wrote about the race on October 6: "The mission of the bicycle is as a practical road vehicle, far more so than a means for a

George E. Weber, at left, riding an American Star Bicycle, lines up for the start of the League of American Wheelman's annual three-mile race on the first day of the Springfield, Massachusetts, Bi-Club Tournament on September 8–10, 1885. Weber won the race in 8 minutes and 34 seconds. Photograph Courtesy of the Burlington County Board of Commissioners/Division of Parks.

sport on the race track, and it is for this reason that such a great interest is taken in a road race. Everyone can ride on a road."¹⁶

The Bicycling World newspaper noted that Weber

> ... is nineteen years of age. His weight is one hundred and fifty-eight pounds, and his height five feet, ten inches. He is well known on the racing field as the rider of a Star, and his recent achievement of making twenty miles within the hour at Springfield is still fresh in the public mind. He has been a rider about a year and a half and out of forty races ridden this year has gained a prize in thirty-six.¹⁷

Weber finished the year with records in the half-mile, the fifteen-mile and the 25-mile races on the track. He also set the American record for most miles (more than twenty) in an hour. He also held the record for the 100-mile road race.

At the end of 1885, things were turning against him and other riders from Smithville within the racing circuit. Editorials in cycling publications and local newspapers stated that Weber was really a professional claiming to be an amateur. In an editorial on July 31, 1885, *The Bicycling World* stated that Weber

> is employed by a bicycle dealer ostensibly as a mechanic. He is on the pay roll of the factory and draws his wages with the mechanics. And yet he never goes to the shop, and he spends all his time on the race track. He is a professional in spirit, though he lives up to the letter of the amateur law. He can join the League (League of American Wheelmen), he can enter amateur events, but others who are more straightforward and come out boldly as professionals are debarred for the League, and they seldom get a chance to race, from the fact that the professional events seldom find a place on race programmes.¹⁸

In England, the Amateur Athletic Club "refused to admit those it classified as 'mechanics, artisans, or labourers' ostensibly because their daily toil gave them an unfair physical advantage."¹⁹ The reality was that

(Left to right) The first prize medal George E. Weber was awarded for winning the 100 Mile Road Race on October 5, 1885, sponsored by the Boston Bicycle Club. The first-place medal awarded to George E. Weber at the National Fifty Mile Road Race held in Clarksville, Missouri, on April 26, 1886. The medal is unusual because it has an image of a Star Bicycle (lower right) on it. The first-place medal awarded to George E. Weber at the League of American Wheelmen 15-mile Championship Race held in Chicago, Illinois on July 25, 1885. Photographs Courtesy of Janice Weber Hoffman.

The H. B. Smith Machine Company of Smithville (Eastampton, Burlington County), New Jersey, built an eleventh-of-a-mile banked track outside the factory to test the Star Bicycles and make improvements. The employees could also use the track for practice. Photograph Courtesy of the Burlington County Board of Commissioners/Division of Parks.

bicycle racing in this era was the purview of "upscale males"[20] or "the son of a rich merchant, who has little else to do but train for racing."[21]

The facts were true for the racers from Smithville. They were sold Star bicycles at reduced prices. The company built a velodrome outside the factory for the workers to train. H. B. Smith "hired racers to compete against the high mount, proving that the Star was at least competitive, if not a superior racing machine."[22] Since racers in the track events could not win money, they were awarded bicycles, medals, cups, guns, tea services and various other non-monetary prizes. Years later, during a lawsuit between George Pressey and the H. B. Smith Machine Company in 1889, executives for the company stated that the company often paid for their riders' entrance fees to races, transportation costs, riders' bicycling suits, room and board at the events, membership in the L.A.W., a trainer to travel with the riders and often rewarded riders for winning races or setting records. One hundred and fifty dollars was paid to George Weber in 1885 for his first-place finish in the 100-mile Road Race in Boston.[23] Numerous riders from Smithville decided at this point to turn professional. Weber did not, but a county directory for 1886 listed Weber's occupation as "bicyclist."[24]

Prior to the 1886 racing season, *The Boston Globe* was still writing about amateur versus professional cyclists on their Editorial pages:

> With all due respect to the dealers, it is hard to understand how a man who is a mechanic or a clerk, with no apparent means of support beyond his salary, can afford either the time or the money to travel from one end of the country to the other throughout the riding season. These men are paid an enormous salary considering the little time they work in the stores or factories, and when they wish to attend a race meeting they are allowed all the time they want without loss of wages. The salary is so large that the racer pays his own expenses, and still has a neat balance for himself, and in this way the dealer is free to swear that he pays the man nothing for racing."[25]

The negative press did not deter Weber. He started the new year by entering a 50-mile road race on April 26, 1886, in Clarksville, Missouri. He and ten other contestants competed on the almost 25-mile loop. Weber finished in three hours, seven minutes and 42½ seconds. "Weber being nearly a half-hour ahead of the record."[26] According to reports, Weber's prizes won at Clarksville amounted to nearly $400 in value.[27]

Weber next traveled to Boston to compete in an even bigger challenge: the famous Corey Hill Climb. The hill was one of the toughest climbs for any high-wheeled bicyclist. The 8.65 percent grade ascent of 199 feet in a length of 2300 feet had defeated many riders in years past. Unfortunately, the week before the hill climb, the L.A.W. Racing Board declared George E. Weber a professional and warned all amateurs not to compete against him or they would lose their amateur status.[28] Fortunately, the hill climb was not a track race sanctioned by the L.A.W., so any riders could compete in the Corey Hill Climb. Weber was not worried by the announcement. He started the climb, and "it was clear to the most inexperienced that Weber was the man and the result showed this to be a fact, he having gone it in the best time on record of 3 minutes, 16⅖ seconds."[29]

By the summer of 1886, Weber found himself back in Smithville after establishing numerous track records, setting new records at the 100-mile race in back-to-back years and just days before setting a new record on the famous Corey Hill Climb in Boston. He had found fame in his field. The H. B. Smith Machine Company was promoting his accomplishments in advertisements seen throughout the country.

He began training for the upcoming national races in Springfield, Massachusetts, in September. He had escaped the controversy that was still raging in the press about amateurs and professionals. The trade magazines were pushing the riders, like Weber, from "maker's amateurs"[30] towards "the professional ranks" where they thought they belonged. "Then let the League (L.A.W.) take the stigma away from professionalism, regulate professional races, admit professionals to the League and we will see races run as they should be, and without the humbug that obtains today."[31]

The Boston Globe stated that summer that

> Weber is enjoying a much-needed rest at Smithville. He will race no more till September. Of all the maker's amateurs Weber is the hardest worked and it is remarkable that he has not 'gone stale' long ere this. Undoubtedly

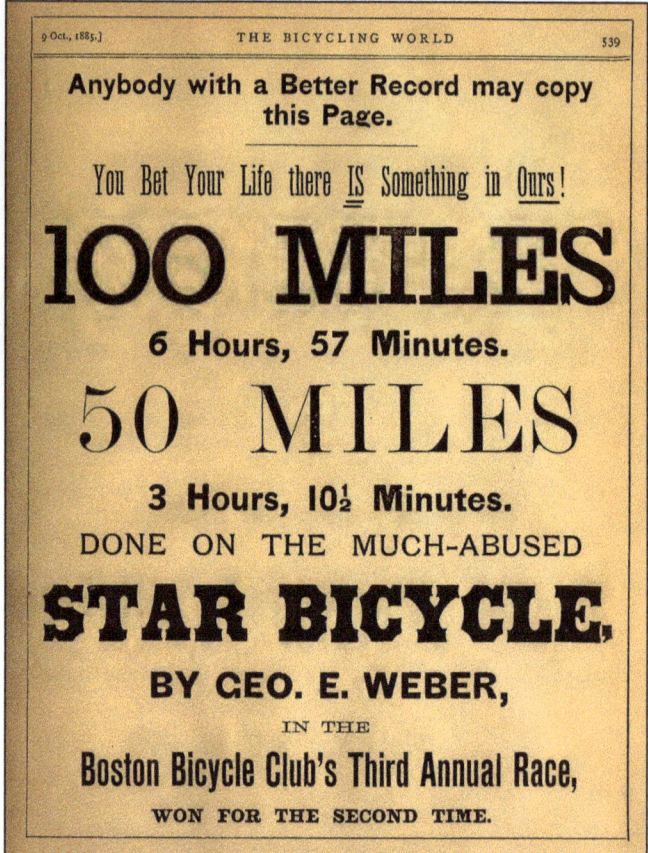

A full page advertisement placed by the H. B. Smith Machine Company in *The Bicycling World* magazine from October 9, 1885, promoting George E. Weber's second consecutive win at the Boston Bicycle Club's 100-mile road race. Image courtesy of the Smithsonian Institute Archives.

> Weber has the strongest physique of any man on the American racing path."[32]

In late July, his trainer, William H. Wallace, noticed "a certain lassitude that was not natural to him.... when beginning to practice for the Springfield Tournament and at the advice of a doctor he was taken off the track and treated for malarial fever."[33] A few weeks later, he felt well enough to take a few laps around the track at Smithville, but his strength had not fully returned. "A day or two later a relapse set in."[34] On Tuesday evening, August 24, at the boarding house where he lived at Smithville, George E. Weber died. He was only twenty years old.

Edward Burns, a fellow employee and Star racer, wrote the next day to Hezekiah Smith, who was away on vacation, "I am very sorry that we have lost another good man, George Weber died last night, from typhoid fever. It is too bad, as nice a young man as could be found anyplace."[35]

> **A Bicyclist Dead.**
> Special Dispatch to THE COURIER.
>
> BURLINGTON, August 25.—George E. Weber, aged 21, the bicycle rider who won several races at Boston, St. Louis and other places, died of typhoid fever at eight o'clock last night at Smithville. He will be buried on Friday from St. Paul's Catholic Church, Burlington. He was sick four weeks.

The Death Notice for George E. Weber appeared in the *Courier-Post* (Camden, New Jersey), August 25, 1886.

Upon hearing about Weber's death, praise came from all parts of the country. *The Bicycling World* stated Weber was "a worthy and upright man, and the greatest Star rider that ever lived."[36] Weber was undoubtedly one of the squarest men who ever raced, and one of the most popular; every one liked George."[37]

His funeral "took place from the residence of his parents in East Burlington, Friday morning, August 27. The remains were conveyed to St. Paul's Roman Catholic Church, where a high Mass of Requiem was celebrated, after which all that was mortal of George E. Weber was laid to rest in the grounds that surround the church."[38]

Without its star rider, the "decline of the Star bicycle"[39] began. Weber's arc matched the high point of the H. B. Smith Machine Company's entrance into the high-wheeled bicycle boom. From the beginning of 1884 through the end of 1886, 70 percent of all Star bicycles were sold,[40] matching Weber's career exactly. No rider in the Star bicycle stable would ever climb to such heights again—nor would the Star bicycle.

About the Author

Dennis McDonald retired from the *Burlington County Times* newspaper after working as a photojournalist for 38 years. During his career at the paper he photographed Carl Lewis, Carli Lloyd, and Franco Harris. His photographs have been published in *Pinelands Folklife*, published by Rutgers University Press, and *Chaseworld: Foxhunting and Storytelling in New Jersey's Pine Barrens,* published by the University of Pennsylvania Press. He has always been interested in local history and has authored two books by Arcadia Publishing on *Medford* and *Smithville*, New Jersey, in the Images of America series. His last story for *SoJourn* was in the premiere issue on the Mount Holly and Smithville Bicycle Railroad. He currently serves on the board of the Whitesbog Preservation Trust.

The author would like to thank Janice Weber Hoffman, Eric Paul Gardner, and Paul W. Schopp for their contributions to this article.

Endnotes

1. "George Weber: Who Rode 100 Miles on the Road in Six Hours and Fifty-seven Minutes," *The Boston Globe*, October 12, 1885.
2. William C. Bolger, *Smithville: The Result of Enterprise* (Mount Holly: Burlington County Cultural & Heritage Commission, 1980), 161.
3. "George Weber: Who Rode 100 Miles."
4. Dennis McDonald, *Images of America: Smithville* (Mount Pleasant: Arcadia Publishing, 2019), 92.
5. McDonald, *Images of America: Smithville*, 91.
6. *Merriam-Webster Dictionary*, www.merriam-webster.com/dictionary.
7. George W. Pressey v. H.B. Smith Machine Company, 139 New Jersey Mirror 1 (N.J.1889).
8. George W. Pressey v. H.B. Smith Machine Company, 139 New Jersey Mirror 1 (N.J.1889).
9. "George Weber: Who Rode 100 Miles."
10. "Racing News: The Capital Club Races," *The Bicycling World*, May 1884, 47.
11. "Philadelphia Tournament," *The Bicycling World* (June 1884): 129.
12. "The Springfield Tournament," *The Bicycling World* (September 1884): 357.
13. "One-Hundred Mile Road Race," *The Bicycling World* (October 1884): 390.
14. "Springfield: The Tournament of 1885," *The Bicycling World* (September 1885): 466.
15. "Boston Century Race," *The Bicycling World* (October 1885): 541.
16. "Weber's Run: He Beats the 100-Mile Road Record," *The Boston Globe*, October 6, 1885.
17. "Boston Century Race," 541.
18. Abbot Bassett, "What is an Amateur?" *The Bicycling World* (July 1885): 279.
19. David V. Herlihy, *Bicycle, The History* (London: Yale University Press, 2004), 197.
20. Herlihy, *Bicycle, The History*, 196.
21. Bassett, "What is an Amateur?" 279.
22. Herlihy, *Bicycle, The History*, 220.
23. George W. Pressey v. H. B. Smith Machine Company, 139 New Jersey Mirror 1 (N.J.1889).
24. *Howe's Burlington County Directory* (Philadelphia: C. E. Howe Company, 1886), 116.
25. "On The Anxious Seat: More Makers' Amateurs in Suspense," *The Boston Globe*, April 4, 1886.
26. "Fifty Mile Road Record Goes," *The Bicycling World* (April 1886): 480.

27 "We Are Told," *The Bicycling World* (May 1886): 51.

28 Abbot Bassett, "More Expulsions and Suspensions," *The Bicycling World* (June 1886): 148.

29 "Corey Hill," *The Bicycling World* (June 1886): 138.

30 Abbot Bassett, "The Amateur Question," *The Bicycling World* (August 1885): 327.

31 Bassett, "The Amateur Question," 327.

32 "Cyclings," *The Boston Globe*, July 18, 1886.

33 "'Star' Weber Dead," *New Haven Daily Morning Journal and Courier*, August 27, 1886.

34 "'Star' Weber Dead."

35 Bolger, *Smithville: The Result of Enterprise*, 164.

36 "All Sorts and Clippings," *The Bicycling World* (September 1886): 446.

37 "News and Opinions: In Brief," *The Bicycling World* (September 1886): 467.

38 "Laid to Rest: Funeral of the Late George E. Weber," *The Wheelman's Gazette* (September 1886): 88.

39 Bolger, *Smithville: The Result of Enterprise*, 164.

40 George W. Pressey v. H. B. Smith Machine Company, 139 New Jersey Mirror 1 (N.J.1889).

Keeping Room, The Franklin Inn, Port Republic. This is where Gary and Nikki Giberson photographed decoys in the extensive collection of Fred Noyes for eventual cataloging. In the previous issue of *SoJourn*, we published an article "Selections from the Noyes Decoy Collection," with captions by Gary Giberson. Judy Courter, author of *Fred and Ethel Noyes of Smithville New Jersey: The Artist and the Entrepreneur*, had the idea for the essay which revisited the once splendid collection. We are very thankful for her excellent idea, encouragement, and support.

South Jersey's Early Scout Hero

Erik L. Burro

It was a mild but heavily overcast day on March 14 in the small river town of Burlington City, New Jersey. The year was 1913, just ten days after the former governor Woodrow Wilson had been inaugurated President. Along West Broad Street, a solid line of wagons, carriages, and automobiles were parked on both sides of the avenue, their occupants already attending a service at St. Mary's Episcopal Church. A black draped hearse was positioned next to the red brick sidewalk closest to the peaked lych gate entry to St. Mary's churchyard. Only a trace of the funeral service could be heard along the street, when the organ and choir swelled to accompany those in attendance.

At the end of the service, a procession emerged from the Gothic sanctuary led by St. Mary's Rev. James Olmsted and assisted by Rev. Philip Smith of nearby St. Barnabas' Church. It was unlike any seen before or since. Family and friends, accompanied by the First and Second troops of Burlington City's Boy Scouts of America, led by scoutmasters Carlton Shoal and William Zelley, followed the casket. The smartly uniformed pall-bearers in their doughboy hats were from the First Troop: Sidney Kaplan and Lewis Levy of the Eagle Patrol, of which the departed had been a member; Edward Johnson and Firman Holland of the Seal Patrol; Thomas Colkitt and Page Scholey of the Wolf Patrol; Robert Taylor and John Gun of the Fox Patrol.

The entourage reverently moved to a gravesite behind the church, near the center of the churchyard. A massive display of floral arrangements from friends, schoolmates, and the community surrounded the mourners. The deceased was fifteen-year-old Scout William S. Bastian, who had died from complications caused by injuries he had sustained the year before. At the same site as his father's grave, who had died when Billy was only four, stood his mother and sister Ruth. As they stepped back from placing their own flowers before the burial, Hillman Conley, Scout trumpeter, stepped forward and sorrowfully played "Taps" while the coffin was lowered into the ground. Among the most distinctive arrangements were flowers creating the first class Scout badge with its banner, "Be Prepared." Already nationally recognized, that same symbol would be permanently etched into the base of the cross-shaped Bastian headstone. As the funeral bell in the spire of St. Mary's began its toll, the entire City of Burlington bid farewell to its Boy Scout hero.

Billy Bastian's gravestone, carved with the Scout symbol on the backside of his deceased father's headstone, beside St. Mary's Episcopal Church, Burlington City.

The year before, also on a Friday, the day after July 4th, Billy and a group of friends were along the riverbank, near the wharf where the ferry regularly arrives and departs. It was a hot summer day so some of the boys decided to take a dip in the river before the ferryboat returned. Although discouraged, it was not that unusual. Local folks often came and went to Burlington Island in their own canoes and rowboats from the nearby shoreline. On weekends and excursion days, the ferry also stopped at Burlington Island, before arriving in Burlington City from Bristol.

Thousands enjoyed Burlington Island's picnic groves and amusement park between 1891 and the 1930s. Steamboat service from Philadelphia, as well as the Burlington-Bristol Ferry, provided access to the island.

It is easy to forget, more than a century ago, how much activity there used to be along Burlington's waterfront. Even in winter, except when occasionally the Delaware River iced over, there was a steady stream of riverine traffic. Steamers moved freight, commercial fisherman set up nets during the early spring, oyster boats delivered fresh harvests from Delaware Bay beginning in October and running through March. Tugboats were constantly seen pushing and pulling barges of coal, sand, and lumber to stops along both sides of the Delaware. Paddlewheel steamers from Philadelphia regularly dropped off and picked up passengers at Burlington and its summer amusement park on Burlington Island, before continuing on to Bristol and sometimes Trenton.

It was customary for all commercial shipping to use shipboard steam whistles that announced their locations along their portions of the channel, often sounding warnings to pleasure boats and fishermen that might be scattered between Burlington, the Burlington Island, and Bristol's busy waterfront. Dockworkers, as well as local boys in Burlington, often gained bragging rights when they could properly identify each of the riverboats by their whistle before coming into view of the Burlington City docks. Experienced listeners recognized the different tones and the subtle length and frequency of each blast, often making it possible to predict not only the riverboat but the captain at the helm. The one steamboat that was heard most frequently each day throughout most of the year was the WILLIAM E. DORON, a small double-ended ferry. It traveled regularly, back and forth with passengers and vehicles, between the diagonally opposite river towns

Ellwood Doron, paddle-wheel ferry model, built in 1864, at boardroom of Bristol's Grundy Memorial Library, which overlooks Burlington Island.

Burlington Waterfront.

of Burlington and Bristol, Pennsylvania. The boat's owner and captain was Billy Doron who had replaced his father's boat, the paddle-wheel ferry ELLWOOD DORON, which had begun making the same crossings after the Civil War.

On the afternoon that Billy Bastian's buddies were swimming at Burlington's harbor, Captain Doron left Bristol, sounding his whistle as he went, clearing the way to Burlington Island and, again, as he approached the island's pier to let off passengers. As he left the island pier, he sounded again, because there were many boaters all around the island enjoying the July 4th weekend. As he rounded the island, he continued his horn blasts, and he began a straight course to the Burlington City dock. The constant ferry tooting was so familiar as background noise to those who lived near the waterfront that Billy Bastian's companions completely ignored the warnings that the William E. Doran was heading their way. The captain, expecting the boys to promptly scurry away, did not immediately reduce speed as he headed for the Burlington ferry slip.

Bastian, seeing his pals were oblivious to the oncoming ferry, ran into the water, shouting and helping each of the unsuspecting swimmers to quickly clamber to safety. As he was last to climb to the top of the landing, the ferry arrived at its slip, with just enough space to clear the youngster. But, at that moment, as Billy reached the top of the pier, the boat bounced off the pilings on the opposite side and came crashing against the pilings where the fifteen year old had sought safety, causing him to be momentarily pinned between the boat and the piling. He struggled free of the boat, withdrew, taking several steps from the edge, then fell to the ground. Local emergency radio and telephone communications were not available, so the boys hurriedly picked him up and carried him off to offices of two different doctors. Neither were home but townspeople caught up with them and rushed the injured boy, by car, to the hospital.

The Burlington Enterprise and Philadelphia's *The Inquirer* both reported Billy Bastian had suffered life threatening injuries. His medical report no longer exists, so we can only guess how long his recovery took. However, later that year, the Burlington Scouts had been invited to participate in a Boy Scouts of America event in Washington, DC. Because they would be staying at a hotel rather than camping, every effort was made to include Billy Bastian on the trip. It began as a steamboat to Philadelphia, where they transferred to an Ericsson Line steamer that left for Baltimore by way of the Chesapeake Canal, and ended with riding a trolley the rest of the way to the nation's capitol. It is not known whether Billy was carried by his fellow scouts, walked with crutches, or was wheelchair bound. Their adventure in the capitol received substantial coverage in the hometown newspaper. It is unknown whether Billy was ever able to return to school, due to his injuries. He died from complications derived from the riverfront accident in March, so his name failed to appear with his class in the Burlington High School yearbook. However, Billy Bastian's heroic action did appear in the national pages of *Boys Life Magazine*, months after it occurred.

As the mourners dispersed along Broad Street, the overcast sky, as if in sympathy with the just-ended

The Ideal Scout statue by Canadian sculptor and University of Pennsylvania Professor Dr. Robert Tait McKenzie, who had been a friend of Baden Powell, the English officer recognized as founder of the Boy Scout movement. McKenzie created his original eighteen-inch bronze in 1915 and presented it to the executive board of the Boy Scouts in Philadelphia where he served as a member for over 20 years. A copy was presented to President Calvin Coolidge at the White House in 1927. Ten years later, he created a life-sized statue and unveiled it at the Philadelphia Boy Scout Headquarters Building. Shown is a bronze copy, one of two in the Garden State, at the Rowan Scouting Resource Center for Burlington Co. Council, Westampton, New Jersey. The other is in Morganville, Marlboro Twp., Monmouth County.

Scout Bastian funeral, rained heavily for the remainder of the day. For more than a century, Burlington and other South Jersey towns have embraced Scouting programs in their communities. This largely forgotten story about one of their early members deserves to be shared with the present generation and is symbolic of the countless ways Scouts like Billy Bastian continue to honor and serve our State and Nation.

ABOUT THE AUTHOR

Erik Burro, a graduate of Rider University, has been active in a broad range of history related activities from America's Bicentennial to present-day commemorations. As a public speaker, he has hosted numerous historic dedications and special events in twelve states, Washington, DC, and five countries. He has addressed the Pennsylvania legislature, multiple times, federal judges at the National Cathedral and been guest lecturer aboard Cunard's transatlantic crossings. Over the years, he has contributed to both news and feature coverage on regional radio and TV, including children's programming, NPR and the BBC.

As both a master of ceremonies and featured performer, Burro has made appearances as famous characters from the past (William Penn, Lord Baltimore, Alexander Hamilton, & others) at conventions, international organizations and cultural societies. Periodically, he is asked to be tour guide/host for visiting trade groups, state officials, and cultural affairs delegations in the tri-state region.

With the unexpected moniker of Monuments Man, he has been recognized for his research, presentations and photo exhibitions on monuments and memorials in and around the Garden State. He continues to initiate awareness of public statues and memorials in need of repair, replacement, or refurbishment and offers resource information and rededication support for their owners.

Burro serves as historian for New Jersey's Heritage Tree Initiative for NJ State Forestry, the restoration of Burlington Island and the New Sweden Center of Colonial History in Delaware. He is founder of Pennjerdel House, a public history advocacy in Burlington, New Jersey. When not preparing lectures for Rutgers and Camden County Community College divisions of Continuing Education, he devotes much of his spare time as a photographer, bibliophile, gardener and occasional writer.

Billy Doron, the last member of the Doron family to operate a ferry service between Burlington and Bristol, discontinued his ferryboat operations the day the contract was signed in 1925 for the new Burlington-Bristol Bridge. Initially funded privately, the Burlington County Bridge Commission operates the toll bridge today. The photograph above shows the diminutive ferryboat WILLIAM E. DORON in her slip in Bristol, Pennsylvania. The boat, built in the yard of Neafie & Levy in the Kensington section of Philadelphia in 1893, still sits at the bottom of the Atlantic Ocean off Virginia as a loss during a storm when being towed to that state from Burlington.

Designated a National Historic Landmark, New St. Mary's Protestant Episcopal Church in Burlington City was designed by architect Richard Upjohn and built between 1846 and 1854. Architect George Wattson Hewitt designed the lych gate at a later date. While the church suffered roof and interior damage during a 1976 fire, the brownstone walls were retained, and restoration was completed in 1981. Modern photographs in this article are by the author.

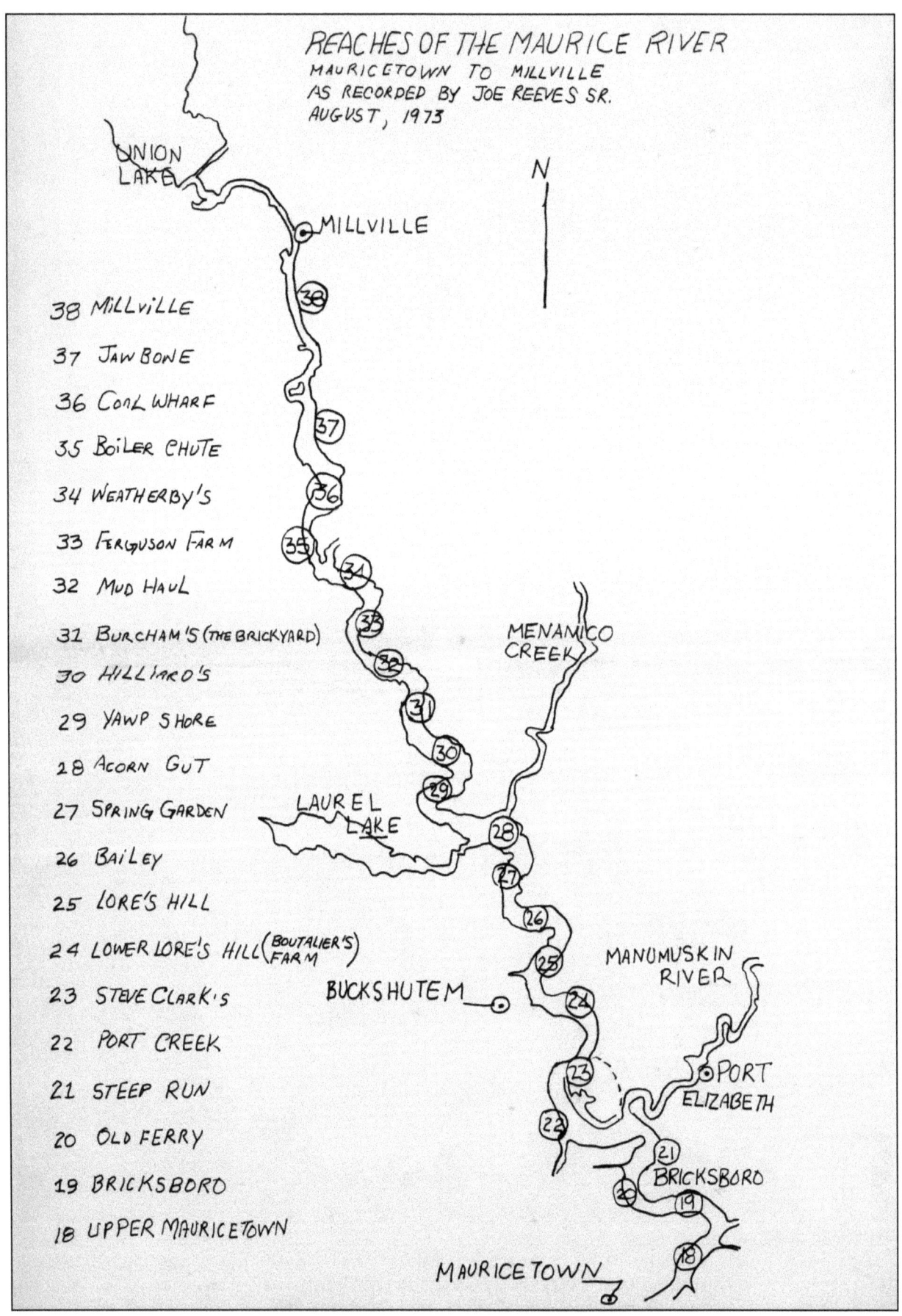

Maurice River Memories:

"Quackam's Beach" and "Relatives"

Joseph S. Reeves Jr.

Quackam's Beach

Mrs. Lizzy Bateman hired me to mow her grass. I asked her for 50 cents but settled for 35. It was my 15th birthday—June 23rd, 1941. A blast from a boat horn downriver sounded for the bridge tender as I finished pushing the mower around the yard for the last turn. I took off, running for the bridge before the second blast came. It was early in the day and the heat hadn't gotten really bad, although I was starting to sweat in the minute or so it took to cover the short distance from the Batemans. The bridge tender, Dewey Stites, was still walking toward the east end of the bridge to put the traffic chain across but I overtook him and did it myself. Only one car was approaching, about a quarter of a mile down the Station Road. Dewey stopped in the center span and took the little round metal cover off the keyway. Then he unbuckled the turning handle from its attachments on the railing. I walked back to the center span, catching my breath, and joined Dewey. We saw Jim Steelman, who had been passing the time of day with Dewey in the tender's shack, fasten the traffic chain across that end as a car was approaching. Harrison Wills came running up the street, jumped over the traffic chain and joined us.

This is the third installment of Joseph S. Reeves Jr.'s stories, first published in his Maurice River Memories *(1993). The work is a collection of his childhood experiences with his family on the Maurice River and shows a bygone era of railbird hunting, fishing, and turtle trapping. These stories are republished in* SoJourn *with the kind permission of the Mauricetown Historical Society, the copyright holder. The accompanying illustrations, including the map to the left, are from the original printing.*

Dewey operated the long lever which raised the latches at each end of the center span, now that the traffic had been halted. Dewey placed the socket of the T-shaped turning arm over the keyway in the center. All three of us pushed hard on the arm and the 150-foot long center span lurched, then started to rotate slowly. The middle section of the trestle bridge moved quite easily after we got it going. Dewey stood to one side while Harrison and I kept walking round in circles while pushing on the arm. The span rotated opposite to the direction we were turning the arm. We could see the big barge which was being pushed upriver by a tug, just keeping steerageway a couple of hundred yards downriver, waiting for us to get the channel clear. Dewey slowed us just before the center span was aligned parallel with the stream. Then it hit the stops gently. The tug's pilot throttled up and the heavy barge started into the draw. It really felt great out here on the bridge, cut off from the town. It was exciting. The barge was loaded with big logs, probably going to the basket factory upriver in Millville. The pilot must have been good, because he didn't have much room to spare. We leaned over the rail and could see only about six feet between the pilings and the hull. There were only two more crewmen on the tug besides the pilot. When the barge cleared we helped Dewey rotate the span back, put the turn arm back in its place, and checked the latch engagements. Then we ran to the ends of the bridge and took down the traffic chains. There were three cars waiting at the east end. In one of them was Mrs. Dunham, my sophomore history teacher in Port Norris High School. She waved to me and I felt pretty good.

I walked up the street with Harrison; he wanted to show me a model airplane he was building. We went into his yard the back way from Stable Lane. Jim and Rose,

75

Harrison's mom and Dad, were home. After I saw his model, I headed back around the church, then decided to go up in the belfry for a look at the area. I'd been up there a couple of times before, so it wasn't anything new. Nobody ever locked the Methodist Church, so I just went in and climbed the stairs. I knew where to go because I had frequently helped my dad when he took care of the furnaces and rang the bells. I took the access door to the belfry and climbed the narrow wooden ladder until I came out in the open alongside the bell. I stepped up on the ladder until I was waist high in the belfry. The view was great from here and there was some breeze blowing. I could see upriver to the reaches near Buckshutem. The barge and tug were just rounding the bend from Upper Mauricetown Reach into Bricksboro Reach. I could see downriver for several reaches and could actually make out the Delaware Bay in the distance. I just stood there awhile and took in the view. I imagined that this is what the view must be like from an airplane. After a time I climbed back down the ladder, left the church and returned to get my lawnmower and collect the 35 cents.

Dad was hanging a carp net out in our side yard. He had driven a 20-penny nail into the corner of the house and had strung the line between it and the old wrought iron hitching post at the corner of the yard. He'd been working at it for several days and had almost finished the 1,200-foot long net. It would be put to use when the season opened on September 1st. Uncle Robert had stopped by and was chatting with my dad about picking up some cedar stakes for carp fishing.

Mom asked me to help her beat out a couple of rugs. I didn't relish the job but said okay and set to it. We took up a rug from the living room and one from a bedroom and draped them over the clothesline. Mom handed me the wire beater and I started whacking the rugs repeatedly. Each blow knocked some dust and grit out. At first, when the rugs still contained a lot of dirt, it kept flying into my eyes and all over me. It would have been better if there had been a breeze blowing. It was hot dirty work, but was the only way to clean rugs. Normally mom worked the rugs over earlier in the spring but we were a bit late this year. After a while, continued beating didn't loosen any

more dirt, so the job was done. I was so dirty I looked like a coal miner.

I decided that as long as I was dirty already I might as well tackle another overdue job. I began cleaning out my chicken coop. I let all the chickens out of the pen. They wouldn't go far but I kept close watch on them anyway. I had about a dozen chickens, mainly Barred Plymouth Rock and Rhode Island Reds. I had a big White Plymouth Rock rooster my sisters and I named "Cockle." He was very territorial and liked to chase anybody he didn't recognize. David Berry came into the yard on his bicycle while I was in the pen working. He didn't see Cockle until it was too late. The rooster charged him and David took off but the bird leaped up and spurred him on the ankle anyway. We shouldn't have thought it funny but my kid sister Louise and I had a good laugh.

During the hot job of cleaning out the coop I was working up a real sweat. It was getting on to late morning and the temperature must have been pushing 90 degrees. I heard kids gathering at Quackums Beach so I went inside, got on my trunks and headed down there.

Quackam Shropshire was the brother of Miss Moseline Shropshire, my grandad's next-door neighbor. After his sister passed away in 1940, Quackam wanted to make a place for kids to swim. His lot backed up on the river alongside my grandad's. The shoreline had been neglected for years. It had even been used to dump trash. Quackam took down the picket fence which bordered Grandad's yard and hired a crew to come in and clean out all the old trash and brush. Then he had truckload after truckload of gravel dumped on the bank. This was topped off with several truckloads of white sand. There was so much sand it even covered some of the mud flat at low tide. The place was immediately named "Quackam's Beach" and became the spot for most of the town kids to swim. Uncle Albert helped by anchoring a big wood float about 30 feet offshore so when the tide went out we still had some depth to the water. You still had to be careful of the bottom because there could be a rusty can or broken bottle in the mud. We kids had swum enough in the Maurice River to be alert for that stuff anyway.

Everyone entered Quackam's by way of Grandad's yard. There was a well-travelled gravel drive down to the river, worn there by trucks coming to buy fish. The tide was just right today. High tide was due about two p.m., so there would be good swimming for hours. Mrs. Camburn and her teenage kids were there. Doris Templin, the preacher's daughter, was too. Just after I arrived, Mellville Burford showed up. Then the Herbert kids came. I didn't waste any time getting into the water. I dove off the shipyard pier and swam out for a distance, then came back and sat on the float. My cousin Robert came in too. At age eleven he was four years my junior so aunt Evelyn always watched while he swam. Mom and dad had watched me as well until just this year. We all dove and swam a lot, pushed each other off the float and generally horsed around. My cousins Norman and Mary Ethel showed up in their suits, accompanied by their mother, Anna. Norman's dad, Uncle Percy, had died last year, a short while after they had moved to Bridgeton. They still missed Mauricetown and came down occasionally to visit.

The water in the river would have been considered too muddy to swim in by a lot of people. It did carry a lot of silt but we thought of it as clean mud. There was no contamination. One drawback was poor visibility underwater. You could only see a foot or two even with bright sunshine. We never gave it a second thought. In fact I always looked forward to summer in the river, since we didn't have running water in our home. I felt much cleaner after a swim. Many times we would take soap and scrub up, followed by a swim to rinse off.

I thought maybe Hazel McAllen, who lived across the street from Grandad, would come in but she never did. Maybe it was that she was embarrassed. Just a few months before I had given her a jewelry box for Valentine's day. I had made the heart-shaped box in Manual Training class. A lot of hard work had gone into it. It was made of clear maple with a hinged walnut lid. In the center of the heart-shaped walnut lid I had inlaid a small maple heart. Within that I had cut an "H" in Old English and filled it with walnut wood filler. After several coats of clear varnish, the jewelry box was a beautiful gift. I was just learning to use the power tools in the shop and really enjoyed the project. Mr. De'Armott, the shop teacher, gave me a good grade for excellent work. A short time after I'd given Hazel the box we broke up. Then, for no apparent reason, she brought the box to the school bus stop one morning. She threw it on the ground in front of all the kids waiting there, lifted her foot and smashed it into a thousand pieces. Hazel was somewhat heavy for her age, so the blow was severe. Actually, I didn't feel all that bad about Hazel, but I sure felt bad about the box. We kept our distance from each other after that.

After an hour or so of swimming, Uncle Jack, who was 20 years old, showed up in his trunks and said he was going to drive to Laurel Lake. There was a mad dash for his car. When we drove away he had a full load and Norman and I were standing on the running boards on either side, hanging on to the window posts. He drove up the street with everyone yelling and screaming and I saw

Mom standing on our front porch with a worried look on her face. We covered the four miles up Buckshutem Road to the lake at a good clip. Jack pulled in at the first open area and we all ran and dove into the cool water. Laurel Lake must have been 10 or 15 degrees cooler than the river; it was a bit of a shock. The lake water was clear and fun to swim in. In only a few minutes all the kids wanted to go back, so we all headed for the car. Some wanted to take the running boards but Norman and I wouldn't give up our spots.

Back at Quackam's Beach, we all dove into the river again. The tide was at peak load and the water felt very warm compared to the lake. My sister Irene and Esther Bradway came around in their suits but they wouldn't swim. Sis had turned sixteen in January and was real conscious of her looks. Esther was closer to my age. They both said they didn't want to get their hair wet. More kids came down and the place turned into a melee of kids pushing each other into the water and creating a lot of noise. This kept up for some time, until the tide dropped, exposing the shoreline. I'd been in the water so much my skin was wrinkled and had been under so much my nose was clogged up with water. The time was getting on to when newspapers had to be delivered anyway so I went back up to the house.

Mom's brother Charlie McClain, Aunt Sarah, and Cousin Vivian had just dropped by for a short visit. They came mainly to see Grandpa and Grandma McClain, who were living with us. Old age and failing health had overtaken them last year and they couldn't be allowed to stay in their home in Leesburg. Mom and her three married brothers had worked out arrangements to take care of my grandparents by rotating them between families every few months. Their care was to be shared equally among the four. No one could afford nursing care. As it turned out, my mom wound up taking them into our home most of the time.

Charlie lived in Woodbury, Gloucester County, so we didn't see him and Aunt Sarah very much. Charlie was an engineer on the Pennsylvania Railroad and he would tell us stories about it sometimes. He started to tell me about how the locomotive used to take on water by scooping it up from a long reservoir between the tracks while the train was doing 70 miles per hour. As Uncle Charlie was getting into the story Sarah, who couldn't sit in one place for more than a few minutes, said they had to go.

I loaded up my newspapers and started delivering. A few kids were still struggling up from Quackam's beach. They always walked in the middle of the paved road because all the sidewalks were gravel and the stones hurt bare feet. It was still hot so I planned on one last swim after I finished the paper route although it was going to be low tide.

Later I was pedaling my bike back to town on the Buckshutem Road after delivering to the last house. A car passed, going about sixty, and almost blew me off the road. I recognized Quackam in his big 1929 Packard straight eight touring car. He was hunched over the steering wheel as though he were in a race. They said he had rolled the car doing eighty a few days ago. Anytime I'd ever been in a car with my uncles we never went faster than 45 miles per hour.

Relatives

My dad, Joe Reeves, was the eldest brother in a large family of brothers and sisters. All the brothers were shad fishermen and when the fish were coming upriver in the spring there were times when they were all out on the river at the same time. The spring shad season was the best time of the year on the Maurice River. From the time I had to enjoy occasional shad fishing with my dad about 1939 until I fished alone in 1943 and 1944 I had looked forward to this time of year. The pace of life was slow and peaceful around Mauricetown then, even after World War II began.

A gentle breeze stirred tiny ripples on the surface as my dad and I drifted up Mauricetown Reach on the last of the flood tide. It was a beautiful spring day on the Maurice River in the second week of May, 1942. From our boat we watched a wavy line of cork floats which suspended a gill net we had been tending after "laying off" down river a half hour before. From the sun's position in the cloudless sky we judged the time to be about ten o'clock. A brief look at the shoreline indicated that our upriver drift had slowed in the last several minutes. We were less than a quarter of a mile south of town and our drift would stop well before the bridge.

Up near town my Uncle Jack Reeves was also drifting for shad. Dad guessed that Jack would probably have to take up his net because the flood tide would last long enough to take him to the bridge. Jack was the youngest of my dad's brothers and would be going into the army soon.

My dad's cousin Harry Reeves (everybody called him Houk, pronounced "How-lk") was taking his net out of the water, way up near the bridge. Just beyond him my Uncle Morty Reeves sat watching from his boat, temporarily moored to a clump of pilings at the south

Maurice River Memories

end of the bridge's east pier. After "taking up" Houk would probably row over and join him; they would wait for the ebb tide to permit downriver drifts. Unspoken river custom dictated that Morty would lay off first and that Houk would have to wait until Morty had drifted downriver several hundred yards before putting his own net back in the river. Morty chewed on an unlit cigar while he watched Houk take in the final few fathoms of his net as he drifted into the draw between the bridge piers.

I looked back downriver and saw my Uncle Robert Reeves drifting up behind us about a quarter of a mile away. I could see him in mid river leaning over the side of his boat taking in a fish. Way down near the point where Mauricetown Reach curves northeastward into Noman's Friend, I could also see Uncle Albert Reeves tending his drift net. I knew it was Albert even at that distance because when we were laying off downriver earlier he was next in line behind Robert.

It was good not to have to take up the drift net for the bridge; we were going to be in luck. Our upriver drift was slowing almost to a stop. We noted a strike about one third the way along the net. I backed the boat over so my dad could reach the bobbing cork float. He eased that section of the net up very gently, reached deep into the water and grasped a five- to six-pound roe shad by the head. It was just barely gilled. A careless pull on the net by a less experienced fisherman would have lost the shad. My dad lowered the net back in the water and placed the fish in a box with a half dozen or so we had caught on this drift.

Our drift had almost stopped, with the net positioned cross-river nearly in line with Stowman's shipyard. A two-masted oyster schooner had been hauled out on the way and the ship's bottom was being scraped, caulked and painted. The sound of mallets on caulking chisels was continuous and rhythmic above the voices of the workmen. The pleasant smell of hot pitch and oakum drifted to us on the light breeze. The old Reeves home where Grandmother Ethel died in 1939 lay on the north boundary of the shipyard. Albert and Jack lived there with

RETURNING WITH THE CATCH - MAY, 1941.

Grandad Morton and conducted fishing, trapping and hunting operations from the wharf and dock on the river. My dad now used the county wharf at the foot of Noble Street, just a stone's throw upriver.

My sister Irene appeared at our wharf and started waving for us to come in. I rowed the short distance over to her and she handed us some food. We had been on the river since six-thirty and were hungry. However, we took this opportunity to carry the eight shad we had caught up to the ice chest in our backyard. We left the wooden box on the boat and carried the fish by hooking our fingers through their gills. They ranged in weight from four to seven pounds. Dad carried five and I took three for the short walk up to the house. Mom and sis were hanging wash on the line. I grabbed a chip of ice from the chest to ease my thirst, then we hurried back down to the boat.

We had caught the peak of the flood tide and the drift net was still motionless on the river. Heading back out to the net we could see a cork bobbing on the far end. My dad said I could take this fish, so he took the oars. He had let me take fish before but I was still gaining experience. This one was well-tangled so there was not much risk of my losing it. I was not taking any chances; I laid the fish and that whole section of net on the boat's stern. I worked on the tangle in that manner instead of holding it over the side as my dad could do. After a few minutes, I boated the fish and got the net back in the water. When I looked up we had started drifting downriver and were already below the shipyard. Mom had made us peanut butter and jelly sandwiches from her homemade wholewheat bread; they really hit the spot.

Up at the bridge, Morty was laying off by passing his net off while his boat was still moored to the pilings at the bridge pier. That was okay, but when his net was all in the water it would be aligned with the current and he would have to tow each end to get it cross-river. An oyster boat was docked at a wharf on the east end of the bridge. Houk was watching from his boat which he had moored to the rigging under the bowsprit of the oyster schooner. He was the only other fisherman waiting to lay off. Jack had rowed in, probably to ice fish or get something to eat while he waited his turn.

We towed our net a bit to get it straightened cross-river. My dad dumped some river water in the boat with the bailer, sloshed it around a bit to loosen fish scales stuck to the boat, then bailed it out, leaving the boat much cleaner. We were drifting downriver faster now and were well below the shipyard. I heard the sound of airplanes and looked up in time to see an Army Air Corps Curtiss P40 War-hawk jump a Navy Grumman F4F Wildcat approaching from the southeast. High overhead the two fighters turned around and around. Their maneuvers gradually took them in a southwesterly direction until they went out of sight. We figured the P40 was from Millville Army Base and the navy plane was probably from Cape May Naval Air Station. I knew the plane types very well because we had been making aircraft models in high school and supplying them to the military (the models were used for recognition training).

When we were well down reach we saw Jack leave his wharf to lay off behind Houk, who had his net in the water. Downriver Albert had drifted out of sight into the next reach. Robert was starting his tow around the bend. The sounds from the shipyard were fading but we could still hear the planks on the bridge clatter when an occasional car passed across them. From our boat the two features of Mauricetown which were most prominent dominated the scene: the trestle bridge and the tall white church steeple.

Several corks went under on the west end of the net. Two of the corks stayed under and for a moment I thought we had struck a fast on the river bottom and were in trouble. Then I realized the tide was still well up and if we had been fast, the whole net would have gone under. When we reached the area where the corks had gone under my dad carefully eased up that section of net and remarked that it did not feel like shad. Soon we saw a large rock (striped bass) well tangled and fighting hard. Dad allowed the fish to dive out of sight a couple of times or it would have torn away from the fine thread net. When it neared the surface again he swung a sharp steel gaff into it just behind the head, then boated it net and all. The rock was more than three feet long and would probably be at least 30 pounds. When we got the fish out of the net and cleared the tangles we could see a fair-sized hole. Dad said he would repair it the next day after we dried the net overnight. We would drift the net for the rest of the day anyway. The big fish thrashed around the boat, splashing us with water which had drained from the tangled net and mixed with blood from the fish.

We had used so much time clearing the rock fish that we had to hurry to the opposite side of the net and start the tow around the bend into Noman's Friend Reach. The ebb tide had not gained full force yet so I stayed on the oars, braced a foot firmly on a support, and rowed hard for the point of the bend with the net in tow.

We were having a good day on the Maurice River.

In Memoriam Mark W. Maxwell

Dennis Niceler & Friends

Mark Maxwell loved history—and he loved Egg Harbor City. In a sense, Mark was a product of the history he so treasured. He was related to many people and knew many more. Some of his relatives owned businesses, and served as well-respected teachers, council members and mayors. He was a lifelong member and Elder of St. John's United Church of Christ. His mother became a Sunday school teacher at St. Johns well before he was born. Mark graduated from Dubuque University with a bachelor's degree in chemistry, and then took a job with the New Jersey State Police as a Forensic Chemist and stuck around for 42 years until his retirement in 2013.

Occasionally, he would tell of his travels as a state expert and how he sometimes sat outside a court room for hours, only to learn that the defendant had pled guilty.

According to Jimmy Maxwell, Mark's youngest son, his Aunt Eileen gave Mark his uncle's pilot logs, which interested him in VF-6. Fighting Squadron 6 or VF-6 was an aviation unit of the United States Navy from 1921 until 1945. The squadron gained fame during World War II. Jimmy's Uncle Bill was a member of the squadron. After Bill's wife gave some squadron mementos to Mark, he contacted a couple of the former members to learn more. This set him on the journey which led to reuniting more and more members. He put together many squadron reunions, the first being in Chicago in May 1989. "It was my dad's first big historian romp—even before the EHCHS," Jimmy remembers.

The Civil War also fascinated Mark, causing him to take the family on trips to Gettysburg and Antietam. But, it was Mark's tenure as President of the Egg Harbor City Historical Society where he really shined. With his ability to give a presentation on Amatol and then oversee a repair at the Roundhouse, Mark seemed to have been destined to guide his hometown historical society.

Mark Maxwell.

Mark understood that history was personal to most people. He had the innate belief that the past often came down to home, school, church and cemetery. Folks came to the Roundhouse Museum in search of their great-grandparents' home, to reminisce about their days at St. Nick's, to learn more about how their parents got together or to come to grips with a death.

Egg Harbor City's history can be so infectious that new residents and contractors alike have come to the Roundhouse to learn more about the homes they have purchased. It was precisely because of this conviction that Mark doggedly created searchable spreadsheets of the city's older tax books. He scanned hundreds of photographs and linked similar images. Along with Ron Hesse and other long-time members of the society, he expended a great deal of time putting names to faces in many a photograph.

Debbie Dellanoce, a founding member and president of the society, remembers Mark grumbling about the handwriting in those tax books. Later, he exclaimed that he had finally figured out the handwriting, but when he turned to another ledger, he had to learn someone else's hand all over.

On a Sunday afternoon in May 2009, Mark called and invited me to the Roundhouse, where he had removed the 1857 color lithograph of Egg Harbor City from its ancient frame to take unfettered photographs. There are only two known copies of this lithograph, one of which belongs to the Egg Harbor City Historical Society and the other to a member of Mark's family.

When the final resting place of Philip Matthias Wolsieffer —a founder of the Gloucester Farm and Town Association and the first mayor of Egg Harbor City—was located, it was Mark who suggested that the society place a headstone on the grave and hold a memorial service. Wolsieffer is the great, great grandfather of Mildred Norman Ryder, Peace Pilgrim, and Helene Young, her sister. Helene was a member of the party that day.

Carl Farrell, Museum Curator of the Hamilton Township Historical Society, recalls Mark as a walking encyclopedia of knowledge on history, forensic science, and even everyday things like fixing a lawn mower. "If he didn't know the answer to a question, he would make it a point to find it," Carl said.

Mark's son Jimmy believes that one of his biggest accomplishments was his work to digitally restore one of the society's Gloucester Farm and Town Association maps. This map was painstakingly "stitched" back into one piece. Progress was often reviewed on Saturday afternoons at the Roundhouse. "He was pumped when he finally got it printed," Jimmy said. The historical society still offers a copy of this map for sale.

Another achievement was the work he did on Find-A-Grave. Jimmy has said that this work was very important to his father, who wound up adding nearly 20,000 memorials to the database. He was the author of *Egg Harbor City*, printed by Arcadia Publishing, as well as named Egg Harbor City Citizen of the Year in 2010.

Mark was a strong-willed person. In October 2014, he discovered that he had myeloma, yet kept up with his historical work. After successful treatment, he went into remission a year later. In August 2020, a bone marrow scan revealed that Mark was free of the myeloma. A short time later, he learned that an opportunistic form of pre-leukemia had begun to affect him, yet he kept on working. He even brought photographs of tax books in order to continue data logging while in hospital isolation that began in February 2021.

Mark passed away on April 22, 2021.
I'll miss him.

Dennis Niceler

(Many thanks to Patty Maxwell, Jimmy Maxwell, Debbie Dellanoce, Carl Farrell and Hazel Mueller for their help.)

Mayor Joseph J. Kuehner Jr. picks the winning ticket at the Egg Harbor City Historical Society's annual dinner meeting at Renault Winery on July 26, 2010.

The Sum of Its Parts:
The Making of Port Republic

Paul W. Schopp

For those folks who have even a modicum of knowledge about northeastern Atlantic County, Port Republic and its environs stand out to many as a community of great antiquity that generates interest and curiosity about its past, a past that stretches back into the early eighteenth century and perhaps beyond. The Leeds and Smith families already owned land in that area during the late seventeenth and into the early eighteenth century. The Port Republic of today, which the New Jersey State Legislature established as a city form of municipal governance in March 1905, erecting the new community's landmass out of Galloway Township,[1] comprises several discreet historic settlements, each of which had its own name. Each of these settlements are discussed below more or less in chronological order. This article is not intended to be a

In this timeless Max Kirscht image, a carriage with its retractable roof deployed drifts up Main Street in Port Republic. In the background is the faint form of the Methodist Church edifice.

full history of Port Republic, but rather to provide an introduction to each of the settlements that historically contributed to create the city of today.

Morss's Mill

Based on documentary research, it appears that Robert Morss Jr. established the first mill—a sawmill—in what would become Port Republic. His mill stood on the north side of Nacote Creek, and Mill Street originally used the milldam as part of its route. Robert Morss Jr. was born c. 1716 to Robert Morse (or Morss) Sr. and his unidentified wife in Elizabeth, Essex County (now Union County), New Jersey. His siblings included his younger brother, Daniel Morse, and Ephraim Morse, Mary Morse, and James Morss, the last-named born about 1730. The Morss family emigrated from Marlborough, Wiltshire, England, and entered the American colonies through New England, landing in Newbury, Essex County, Massachusetts.[2]

Robert Morss Jr. apparently relocated from Elizabethtown to Burlington County. There, he married Jemima Wood, of Burlington County, sometime in the third or fourth decade of the eighteenth century. The couple subsequently filed their marriage documents with the colonial government on September 15, 1741.[3] Jemima Wood was the daughter of Jonas Wood, who also settled in Elizabethtown. Friendly with the Morss family, Wood also engaged in speculative land purchases with Robert Morss Sr., including a 60-acre parcel near Chestnut Neck, surveyed to them on October 27, 1729.[4] Another daughter of Jonas Wood—Elizabeth—wedded Nehemiah Leeds of Leeds Point. The couple submitted their marriage documents to the colonial government on September 24, 1735.[5] It appears Robert and Jemima

In another Max Kirscht view, the 1774 gristmill can be seen on the left with what appear to be several Boling Settlement residents standing in front. On the right is the store and post office building that first housed the Gravelly Landing Post Office beginning in 1827. By this time, the gristmill had long fallen out of use and it sat derelict until it was demolished prior to 1925. Likewise, the windows on the store's first floor are boarded over, indicating the store had permanently closed.

The Making of Port Republic

relocated to present-day Galloway Township, Gloucester County soon after their marriage, where their children were all born: Rebecca, Joshua, Nicholas, Nehemiah, and Jonas. Morss was already living in Galloway before January 1745, when his name appears as a debtor in the estate inventory of Amos Ireland.[6]

It is unclear when Morss first erected his sawmill, but he likely did so soon after arriving in what would become Galloway Township. During Robert Morss's ownership, the locality naturally carried the name of "Morss's Mill," which eventually morphed into "Moss Mill."

Clark's Mill

Morss sold his first sawmill to brothers Thomas and David Clark prior to October 1774 (and likely in the 1760s) and moved his sawyer operations up the Morss Mill Branch of Nacote Creek.[7] As a result of the sale to the Clark brothers, the settlement soon went by the name "Clark's Mill, while another toponym applied to the area was "Wrangleboro(ugh)." The folklore surrounding this name suggests that the men living there always stood ready to fight all-comers, but such an account seems preposterous on its face. Consultation of the *Oxford English Dictionary* reveals that a wrangle, or more properly, a wrangel, is defined as "The rib of a boat."[8] Given the number of shipyards/boatyards along the Mullica and elsewhere in coastal southern New Jersey, it makes sense that at least some local sawmills engaged in servicing those yards with such components. Hence, the area likely received the name Wrangleboro to indicate the products it generated. In Thomas F. Gordon's 1834 *Gazetteer of the State of New Jersey*, he records this place name as:

> *Wrangleboro or Clark's Mill*, village, on Nacote creek, of Galloway t-ship, Gloucester co., about 37 miles S. E. from Woodbury; contains a store, one or more taverns, and one mill, and 15 or 20 dwellings.[9]

Following Morss selling his mill to Thomas and David Clark, the area became known as Clark's Mill or Wrangleboro as noted in the quote from Gordon's gazetteer. A charter granted in 1774 allowed Evi Smith, Hugh McCollum, and Richard Westcoat to erect a dam across Nacote Creek. The men proceeded to erect the gristmill mentioned in Gordon's description proximate to the Clark sawmill. The gristmill had disappeared from the riverbank prior to 1925.

Port Republic

The earliest mention found to-date of Port Republic as a place name in print appears in an April 1814 newspaper advertisement for selling land, which Adrial Clark, owner of the mills there, placed in the April 29, 1814, edition of *The Democratic Press*, a daily newspaper published in Philadelphia at that time.[10] Clark's use of the place name "Port Republic" strongly suggests that the toponym had already entered the areal lexicon at some indeterminant prior time. Although Gordon provides an entry in his 1834 gazetteer for Wrangleboro, yet he fails to mention Port Republic, some twenty years after Clark placed his land sale advertisement. Instead of including Port Republic, Gordon published an entry for Gravelly Landing, of which he notes,

> *Gravelly Landing*, p-t. of Galloway t-ship, Gloucester co., 40 miles S. E. from Woodbury, 79 from Trenton, and 187 N. E. from W. C., on Nacote creek, contains a tavern, store, and 10 or 12 dwellings.[11]

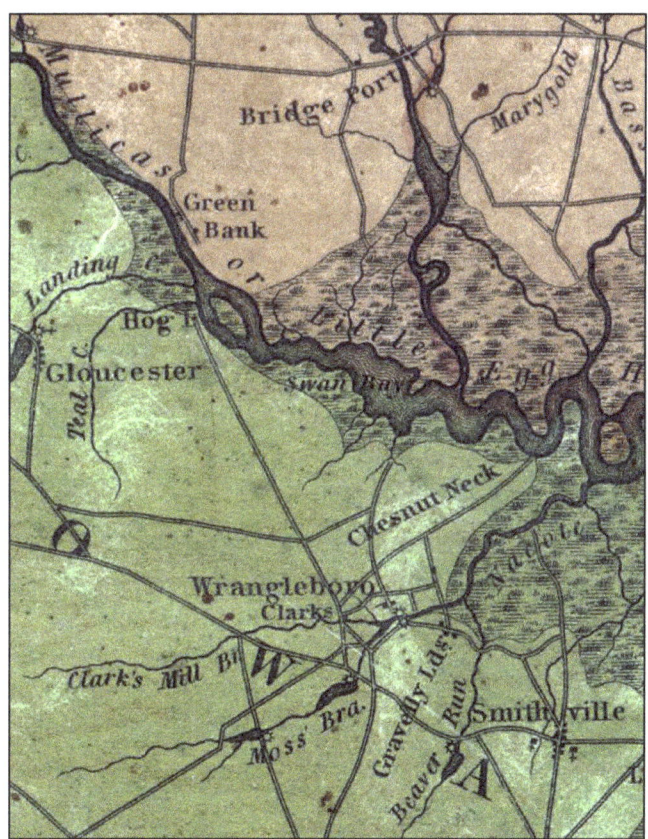

A detail from Thomas Gordon's highly accurate 1828 map of New Jersey showing the early settlements that comprise today's Port Republic, including Wrangleboro, Clarks (Mill), and Gravelly Landing.[12]

When you blend the gazetteer description of Wrangleboro and Gravelly Landing, it creates a satisfactory description of Port Republic as it existed at that time. Thomas Gordon (unrelated to the gazetteer publisher), on his 1828 map of New Jersey, depicts Gravelly Landing as located on the easterly side of Nacote Creek, but the gazetteer description clearly indicates Gravelly Run was a post-town, i.e., it had a post office. Since the only known post office at that time stood near the old gristmill on the westerly side of Nacote Creek, the gazetteer description clearly spans the creek, and it forms the easterly section of the village traditionally known as Port Republic. The Gravelly Landing Post Office opened within the store near the 1774 gristmill on December 18, 1827, with Gilbert Hatfield, the storeowner, serving as the first postmaster.[13] The office continued to operate through the 1837 erection of Atlantic County and then formally changed names to Port Republic on July 28, 1840, with John Endicott as postmaster.[14]

Unionville

Samuel Van Sant, a local farmer and shipbuilder on Nacote Creek, reputedly circulated a petition among the citizenry in 1842 to change the name of Wrangleboro to Unionville.[15] While it is possible Van Sant sought to exhibit some national pride, he more likely derived the name from the local Methodist meeting house, then known as Union Chapel. Micajah Smith constructed the edifice in 1800, first known as Smith's Meeting House; a burial ground still marks the location. Writing in 1916, Anna C. Collins Fleming provides a description of the church:

> The meeting house was a two-story frame building, 25 feet square. It was never dedicated, but as soon as weatherboarded, meetings were held in it in the summer, but in the winter for several years services were held in the upper room of Nehemiah Blackman's house. In 1809 windows were put in and a ten-plate stove purchased. The house was never plastered but was ceiled up with boards. In 1812 they purchased planed boards and had benches made with pieces across the back to rest the shoulder. Their lights were tallow dips, in tin candle sticks. The traveling preacher came once in four weeks and even then could not always make his appointment, and the local preachers, exhorters and class leaders had to take charge a large share of the time.[16]

To Iron Ore Manufacturers!

FOR SALE
A VALUABLE PROPERTY,
SITUATE in Galloway Township, Great Egg Harbor—consisting of Iron Ore, Cedar Swamp, Bank Meadow, Pine Land, &c.

10,000 acres of Pine Lands,
Containing Iron Ore, with streams of water advantageously situate for a Furnace and Forge—The Ore will be *warranted* adequate to keep a Furnace 3 years in blast—and it is expected the supply cannot be exhausted

The above will be sold with or without the following described property.

1st. That noted Stand, Plantation and Saw mill where the subscriber now lives and the Indian-cabin mill, &c 7 miles distant.
2d. 25 acres of excellent well situated meadow in good banks on Nacott creek, with 17 acres of first quality Salt meadow adjoining.
3d. 500 acres valuable growing Cedar Swamp, of which 20 acres is fit to work
4th. 300 acres uncultivated fresh meadow of excellent quality, well situated for banking
5th. 20 acres of arable Land adjacent to Port Republic, pleasantly situate and much improved by a landing for the exportation of Lumber and Receiving of Goods, &c.
6th. 70 acres good salt meadow on Perch cove.
7th. 60 acres good salt meadow on Landing creek and the great Bay, and near to Leed's Point
8th. 55 acres of good Salt meadow and a fine fishery thereon.

All the above tracts are situate on Mullica's river, Nacott creek, and other navigable waters—and can boast of being more advantageously siuated (being nigh the best inlet) than any other property along the seaboard from Delaware to Sandy Hook.

Terms of payment will be made easy and the property will be sold in whole or in part—a *half* or one *fourth* would be preferred to be retained. Application to be made to the Proprietor on the premises, or by letters post paid to care of John F. Watson, Philadelphia.

Adriah Clark.

Rptd 9—f n2:

A facsimile of the original advertisement that appeared in the April 29, 1814, edition of *The Democratic Press*, published in Philadelphia. Item 5 in the sale notice contains the earliest published use of the name Port Republic.

The Making of Port Republic

The vignette map of Port Republic from the Beers' 1872 *Topographical Map of Atlantic Co. New Jersey* that demonstrates a more unified nucleated village incorporating Wrangleboro, Clarks Mill, Unionville, and Gravelly Landing. At the time, David Somers Blackman owned the mill complex at the mill pond seen on the lower left. R. M. Ashley owned the brick store that housed the Gravelly Run Post Office beginning in 1827 and the 1774 gristmill sits just below the store, supplanted by a new gristmill east of Mill Street. As noted on the map, Port Republic had two schools, School No. 5 and School No. 7. The latter school stood in what had been Gravelly Landing and School No. 5 was located in what had been Unionville. Children from the Boling Settlement attended School No. 5.[17]

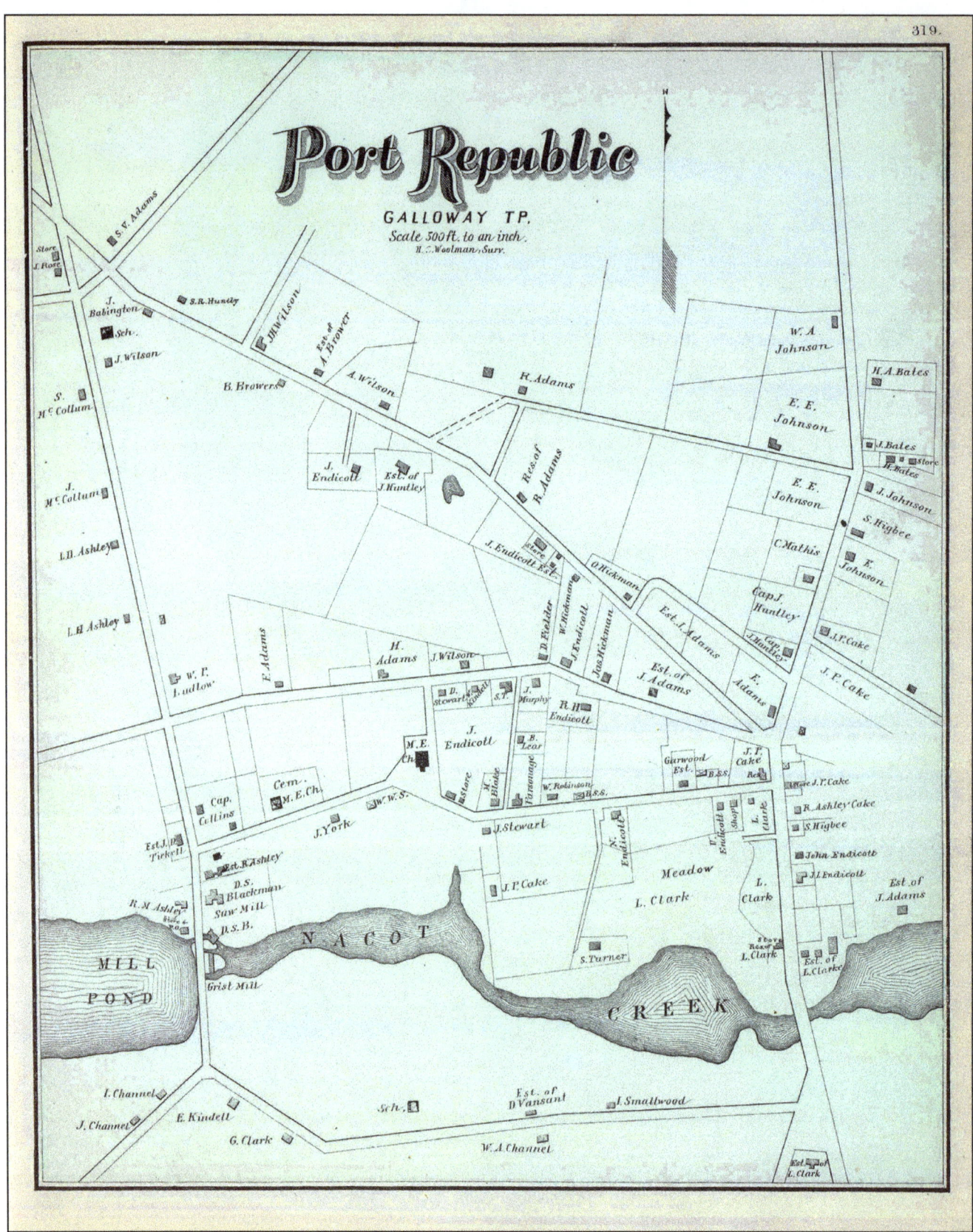

This 1878 map appears in the famous Woolman and Rose atlas of coastal New Jersey. While its similarities with the 1872 vignette map are striking, there are enough differences to make this second 1870s map of Port Republic useful to include with this article. A study of the two maps will reveal additional streets, wider coverage, and more residences on the map above.[18]

The Making of Port Republic

The earliest use of Unionville in print found to-date appeared in the February 9, 1853, issue of the *State Gazette* (Trenton), in a brief article describing the death of Captain Samuel Cavalier, who drowned "... near Unionville, Atlantic Co...."[19] Whether the story of Van Sant and the name-change petition is true or apocryphal remains to be seen. It is usually a story associated with locals seeking a post office by that name, but other Unionville communities existed in New Jersey and Pennsylvania, making the potential for mail delivery confusing. Furthermore, the Gravelly Landing Post Office had changed names to become the Port Republic postal facility in July 1840, two years earlier. If Van Sant did, indeed, circulate a petition on a local level in 1842, then he probably just wanted to rid the community of the Wrangleboro moniker and he most likely derived the name Unionville from the old Union Chapel.

Port Republic (continued)

It is unclear how the name "Port Republic" was chosen, but clearly the community existed under that name for more than 25 years before the Gravelly Landing Post Office renaming occurred to become the Port Republic office. It might just stem from the local environs' military involvement during the Revolutionary War, which resulted in creating the republic form of government the nation retains today. By 1850, Port Republic, as the sum of its parts at that time, had grown into a rather busy and respectable community, as the table to the right illustrates:[20]

Professions and Businesses in Port Republic, 1850	
Builders	Merchants (Dry Goods and Groceries)
Adam Conover	Cake & Ashley
Joseph Kindle	J. P. Cake
Daniel Lacey	Peter Lane
	Thomas Clark
Blacksmiths	Lewis Clark
Charles Matthews	Josiah Carter
Boot & Shoemakers	Physicians
C. S. Fries	Dr. Parker
John R. Baxter	
	Shipbuilders
Harness Makers	Josiah Carter
John R. Baxter	Peter Lane
	O. P. Hickman
Mills (Flour & Feed)	Z. Stillman
David Blackman	James Van Zant
A. Doughty	Joel Van Zant
	Daniel Van Zant
Mills (Saw)	
David S. Blackman	Tavern/Hotel Keepers
A. Doughty	Ralph Ashley, Temperance House
Enoch Doughty	
	Wheelwrights
	Thomas Clark
Source: *Kirkbride's New Jersey Business Directory*, 1850, 120–22.	

Photograph of Micajah Smith's grave in the Smith's Meeting House burial ground. Photographed January 22, 2022.

Port Republic hosted six mercantile stores, a total of five mills (grist and saw), and seven shipbuilders within its surrounds. It is likely not all these men had their own shipyards but worked for the several local yard owners. The Van Zant (or Van Sant) family had long engaged in building ships and boats of all descriptions up and down the coastal zone, so it not surprising that three family members constructed vessels at Port Republic.

These two postcard views depict the Van Sant shipyard in Port Republic. Located in a cut along Nacote Creek's northerly bank near the Port Republic Methodist Church, the yard constructed a wide variety of ships, boats, and small craft, ranging from sloops and multi-masted schooners to sneakboxes and garveys. Houseboats and wide workboats tied up the bank can be seen in the upper image. The yard began building boats in the nineteenth century and continued into the twentieth century. The Mullica River can be seen to the right on the upper photo. The small barn-like structure served as a workshop. The natural slope of the bank accommodated the launching of vessels. On the extreme right in the lower image can be seen a small craft under construction in front of the workshop. Set up on stocks, the ribs are in place but not yet trimmed even with the top of the gunwale.

Two more postcard views of the Van Sant shipyard, with the upper image clearly placing the yard geographically on the landscape. The lower image provides some idea of the yard's productivity during the early twentieth century and also just the shear range in types of vessels built.

The Boling Settlement

The Boling Settlement was the final enclave to form a segment of present-day Port Republic, and of all the discreet communities that comprise Port Republic, the Boling Settlement is the only one not identified on the 1872 F. W. Beers' *Topographical Map of Atlantic Co. New Jersey*.[17] For those, however, with a discerning eye, a close examination of the map will reveal its location through the presence of an African Methodist Episcopal Church. Henry and Grace Boling founded the Boling Settlement (c.1857–c.1920), and the settlement quickly grew to include many members of their family, as well as members of the Trusty and Smith families. Over the subsequent four generations, at least forty members of these families lived and worked this land, erected a church upon it, and some are buried beneath its sod.

Henry Boling, the patriarch of the Boling Family, was born c. 1790 in Pennsylvania. By 1830, he and his wife, Grace (c. 1810–1885), were enumerated among the "Free Colored People" of Hamilton Township, Gloucester County, New Jersey.[21] Ten years later, the couple had relocated to Deptford Township, Gloucester County, near the boundary of present-day East Greenwich Township where Kings Highway crosses Mantua Creek, based on the 1849 map of Salem and Gloucester counties.[22, 23] Having moved to Port Republic in 1849, the Boling family lived on or near the land that would become the future Black enclave, but it was not until 1857 that Henry acquired his first piece of land for $32.25, formally founding the Boling Settlement. The 1850 federal decennial census enumerates the Boling household as including Henry, Grace, and their children: Deborah, Sarah, Charles, Rebecca, Beulah, Eli, and Mary.[24] Josiah was probably a nephew.[25]

The Underground Railroad provided a crucial method for moving runaway slaves escaping to the Northern states. Considering its many routes and secretive nature, it is impossible to ascertain a complete

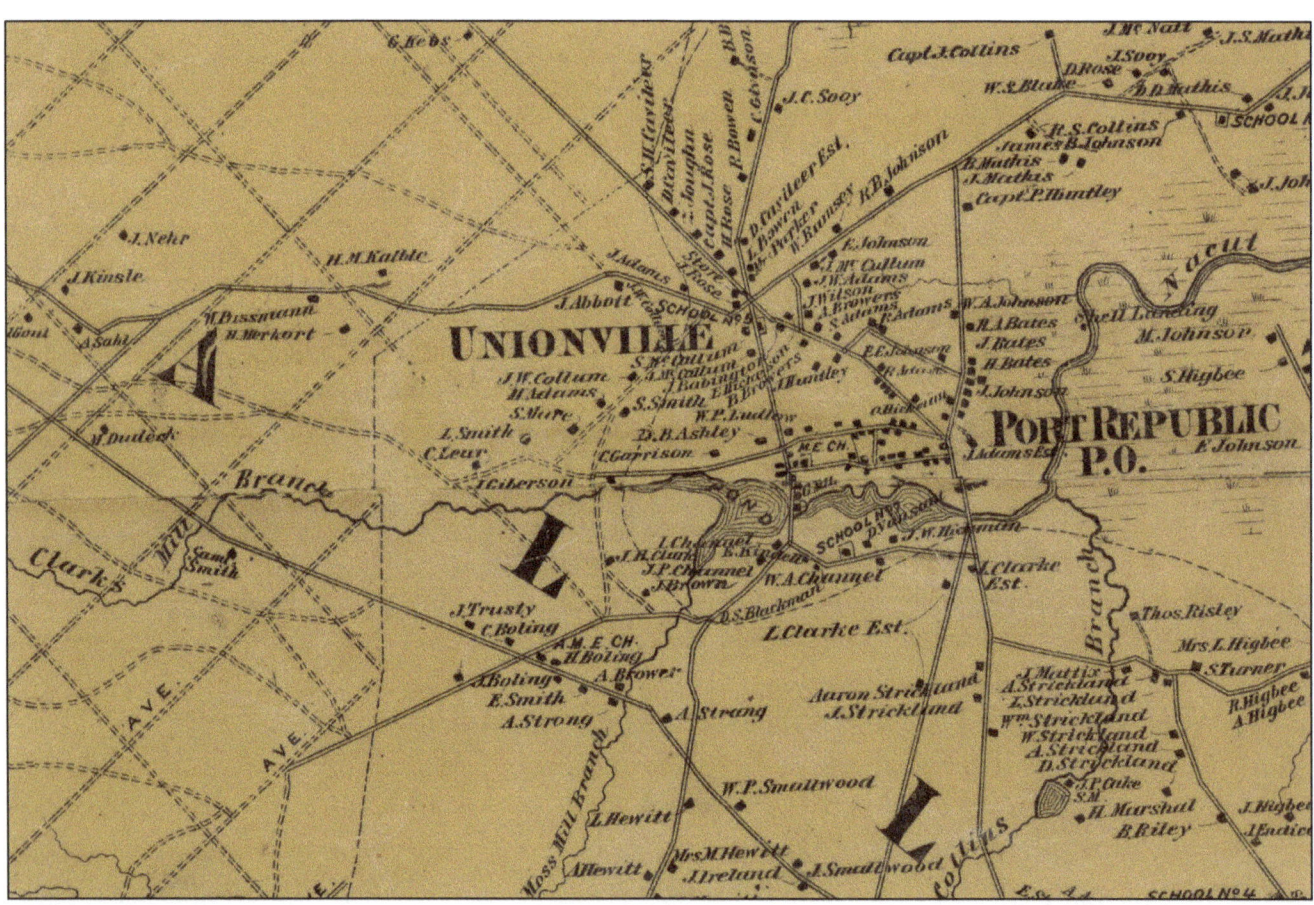

A detail from Beer's 1872 map of Atlantic County, the only two place names identified are Port Republic and Unionville. While the Boling Settlement is not labeled as such, you can observe the Boling, Smith, and Trusty surnames on the lower center portion of the map, along with the "A.M.E. Ch." Surnames on this map read like a who's who of the Mullica River and its banks: Johnson, Mathis, Cavileer, Sooy, Adams, Giberson, Clark, and Bowen. Notice "Shell Landing" before the first oxbow turn on Nacote Creek east of the village. This landing likely served the bog iron industry when the furnaces were in blast. Shells provided the iron works with a type of flux to release dross from the molten ore.

account of its history. According to Emma Marie Trusty, writing in her 1999 Underground Railroad book, the Bolings and the Trustys were important figures in the Underground Railroad in southern New Jersey as early as the 1830s.[26]

Joseph Trusty, father of James Trusty who married Margaret Boling, and his brother Alexander Trusty, father of Ann Eliza Trusty who married Charles Boling, began their work in the Underground Railroad around 1830. Joseph, while still in his early twenties, would bring fugitive slaves across the Delaware Bay by boat. This coincided with his growing interest in religion. Joseph Trusty founded the Bethel African Methodist Episcopal Church, Springtown, New Jersey; oral histories relate that this edifice served as one of the stations Harriet Tubman used from 1849 until 1853. Upon his relocation to Atlantic County around 1840, Joseph became "the key agent" for the Underground Railroad in that area.

Emma Marie Trusty indicates that Henry and Grace Boling hid fugitive slaves in the Boling Settlement as they made their way to Tuckerton, north of the Mullica River. Prior to 1860, James and Margaret Trusty relocated their family to the Boling Settlement, possibly to aid in Underground Railroad operations. When old enough, Charles and Eli Boling also helped, leading runaway slaves through the upper leg of the Mullica Township route. Although it is difficult to know the exact role individuals played, evidence points to the Bolings and Trustys aiding fugitive enslaved persons over the decades.[27]

By the late eighteenth century, Methodists of African descent regularly faced discrimination and racism from white worshipers, prompting a widespread desire among the black community for religious autonomy. Unwilling to stop practicing their faith, many African Americans followed Richard Allen and Absalom Jones in their quest to form a new denomination: the African Methodist Episcopal (AME) Church. Denominational development was generally restricted to the Northeast and Midwest during the antebellum period; as the Civil War engulfed the nation, however, the AME Church's influence quickly spread throughout all parts of the Union.

As members of the Boling Settlement grew increasingly weary of traveling far distances to attend

Although it is in rather sad condition, this is a rare Max Kirscht postcard view of the school and its classes including one Black child from the Boling Settlement, seen all the way on the right. This is School No. 5 in what had been Unionville. As easily seen, the school accommodated classes from the first grade through high school, based on the ages of the students present.

church services, in June 1863 they began construction of their own house of worship, the Ebenezer African Methodist Episcopal Church and the finished the edifice in October.[28] Two parcels of land were utilized, one located at the intersection of Mays Landing and Moss Mill Roads (present: Riverside Drive and Moss Mill Road intersection), and a second, smaller lot, adjacent to the north of the first property and on the south side of Riverside Drive. Total size of the church property was .64 acres. Josiah Boling, Charles Boling, James Trusty, Alexander Smith, Moses Miller, John Romer, and Samuel Smith served as the initial board of trustees.[29] The associated cemetery stands today as the last physical presence of the Boling Settlement.

When services at the Ebenezer AME Church began, there were approximately eight regular church members and five probationers. But after five members of the Boling Settlement enlisted to serve in the Union army the following year, church attendance remained limited until the war's end.[30] Presumably, prospects for the small Port Republic church subsequently picked up in the following years, especially after being inducted into various church circuits in the South Jersey area in the 1870s. Some of the earliest leaders of the Ebenezer AME Church included Pastor John Lukins, who served until his death in 1869; the Reverend Walter Thompson, who began preaching in 1873; and A. H. Brown, who joined in 1874.[31]

Although no records have been identified that indicate when services at the church ended, it is possible to conclude that they stopped within the first two decades of the twentieth century. The building itself seems to have been demolished sometime between 1916, the year in which Charles Boling died and was interred in the adjacent burying ground, and 1931, when a review of aerial photographs revealed no remaining buildings within the Boling Settlement.

A view of all that remains of the Boling Settlement: the Ebenezer A.M.E. Church burying ground, which contains three veteran grave markers to honor those local residents who fought in the U.S.C.I., 25th Regiment and were interred herein.

The Making of Port Republic

Port Republic (concluded)

The settlements that combined to create modern-day Port Republic continued to grow during the second half of the nineteenth century and through the twentieth century. Most of these settlements yielded their individual identity in creating the city, while others like the Boling Settlement, simply disappeared, leaving only its burial ground to indicate it once existed. The maps from 1872 and 1878 visually demonstrate the growth of Port Republic during the nineteenth century, but the city still features many of its historic buildings and residences, giving it a look of antiquity. The beautiful Methodist Church, built in 1871, replaced the Union Chapel edifice. The shipyards are gone, but evidence of their presence can still be found along the shores of Nacote Creek today in the form of bank cuts lined with wharfage boards.

Conclusion

While the full history of Port Republic is much larger story, the purpose of this article was to provide documentation on the various historic settlements that lie or partially lie within the current bounds of the city and help comprise modern-day Port Republic. The editors of *SoJourn* would welcome a comprehensive history of the city to be published in a future issue. The pamphlet issued for the New Jersey's tercentenary in 1964 is the only standalone published account of the city available to date. Perhaps this abbreviated text will lead others to continue researching the community.

The Port Republic stage awaits some traveling members of the public. Meanwhile, Max Kirscht loaded the stage with local children in a posed view. The relaxed driver was obviously amenable to having the young people occupy his stage for the photograph. Max Kirscht was an area photographer who produced a large number of real photo postcards, primarily in Galloway Township, Absecon, Pleasantville, and Egg Harbor City. He maintained a studio in Pleasantville at 7 North Main Street. His father, Herman, also produced photo cards of Port Republic.

Historic and current photographs of the edifice built as the Port Republic Methodist Episcopal Church in 1871. A comparison of the two images allows the viewer to understand the changes that occurred over time, including the all-white paint applied to the exterior. The current congregation separated from the New Jersey Annual Conference in the last few years over doctrinal differences and the church is now known as the Port Republic Community Church.

About this Essay and the Author

The idea for this essay derives from one of the editors remembering an exhibition that Stockton students completed in 2013. The exhibition on the *Boling Settlement of Port Republic* can be found here: https://blogs.stockton.edu/bolingsettlement/. Initial research on the Boling family was completed by Professor Wendel White who generously allowed Kevin M. Konrad and Jesse Kraft, two students in Stockton's American Studies masters program, to use his work as their primary resource. In 2021, Alison Roemer and Elena Gonzalez, two editing interns, returned to the exhibition text for possible reuse. Ultimately, the decision was made to broaden the scope to include all of Port Republic. Paul W. Schopp, Assistant Director of the South Jersey Culture & History Center, agreed to write an introduction to this fascinating place.

Endnotes

1. John P. Snyder, *The Story of New Jersey's Civil Boundaries* (Trenton, NJ: The Bureau of Geology and Topography, 1969, 70.
2. Paul W. Schopp, Research in process.
3. Marriage bonds and licenses, 1727–1734. Secretary of State record group. New Jersey State Archives, Trenton, NJ, 1741, 68.
4. West New Jersey Surveyor General's Office, Survey Book H, now deposited at the New Jersey State Archives, 1729, 460.
5. Marriage bonds and licenses, 1735, 8.
6. A. Van Doren Honeyman, ed., *Documents Relating to the Colonial History of the State of New Jersey, First Series, Vol. XXX, Calendar of New Jersey Wills, Administrations, Etc., Volume II—1730–1750* (Somerville, NJ: The Unionist-Gazette Association). 1913, 259.

7 As indicated in David S. Blackman's survey abstract book, manuscript, private collection, 1866, 140.
8 *Oxford English Dictionary*, online edition. Found at oed.com.
9 Thomas F. Gordon, *Gazetteer of the State of New Jersey* (Trenton, NJ: Daniel Fenton), 1834, 266.
10 "To Iron Ore Manufacturers!" published in the April 29, 1814, edition of *The Democratic Press*, microform edition (Philadelphia, PA: The Democratic Press, 1814, 3.
11 Ibid., 150.
12 Thomas Gordon, *A Map of the State of New Jersey with Part of the Adjoining States* (n.p.), 1828.
13 John L. Kay and Chester M. Smith Jr., *New Jersey Postal History* (Lawrence, MA: Quarterman Publications, Inc.), 1977, 28.
14 Ibid., 29.
15 National Register of Historic Places nomination document for Port Republic Historic District, p. 8-2. Department of the Interior, National Park Service, Washington, D.C. The nomination's author failed to provide a citation for the Van Sant story.
16 Anna S. Collins Fleming, "M.E. Church in Port Republic." Published in *Early History of Atlantic County, New Jersey* (Somers Point, NJ: Atlantic County Historical Society), 1915, 124–25.
17 F. W. Beers, *Topographical Map of Atlantic Co. New Jersey . . .* (New York City, NY: Beers, Comstock & Cline), 1872.
18 H. C. Woolman and T. F. Rose, *Historical and Biographical Atlas of the New Jersey Coast. . . .* (Philadelphia, PA: Woolman & Rose), 1878, 310.
19 "Melancholy Case of Drowning." Published in the February 9, 1853, edition of the *State Gazette*, Microform edition (Trenton, NJ: State Gazette), 1853, 2.
20 Stacy B. Kirkbride Jr., *Kirkbride's New Jersey Business Directory . . .* (Trenton, NJ: n.p.), 1850, 120–22.
21 Fifth federal decennial census, Hamilton Township, Gloucester County, New Jersey. Microform, Series M19, roll 81, 1830, 170.
22 Sixth federal decennial census, Deptford, Gloucester County, New Jersey. Microform, Series M704, roll 252, 1840, 82.
23 Alexander C. Stansbie, James Keily, and Samuel M. Rea, *A Map of the Counties of Salem and Gloucester New Jersey* (Philadelphia, PA: Smith & Wistar, 1849.
24 Seventh federal decennial census, Galloway Township, Atlantic County, New Jersey. Microform, Series M432, roll 442, 1850, 54b.
25 Emma Marie Trusty, *The Underground Railroad Unveiled: Ties That Bound* (Philadelphia, PA: Amed Literary), 1999, 254.
26 Ibid., 246–48.
27 Ibid., 248–56.
28 "For the Christian Recorder." Published in the April 9, 1864, edition of *The Christian Recorder* (Philadelphia, PA: The African American Methodist Church), 59.
29 Deed, "Rollin M. Ashley to Trustees of Ebenezer A.M.E. Church, recorded March 18, 1870, Atlantic County Deed Book 27, 402.
30 "For the Christian Recorder."
31 Joseph H. Morgan, *Morgan's History of the New Jersey Conference of the A.M.E. Church, from 1872 to 1887 . .* (Camden, N.J.: S. Chew, Printer, Front and Market Streets. 1887).

The movable iron pony truss bridge over Nacote Creek carrying Atlantic County Route 610 (Smithville-Port Republic Road). The span is currently undergoing replacement and the bridge is closed until completion. Note the large two-masted schooner tied up adjacent to the bridge and the four men navigating what appears to be a sneakbox under the bridge.

SoJourn
Call for Articles

The South Jersey Culture & History Center at Stockton University publishes twice yearly issues of *SoJourn*. We actively seek community members, avocational historians, and scholars to contribute essays on topics related to South Jersey. Illustrations to accompany these articles will be a plus. Articles should be written for laypersons who are interested and curious about South Jersey topics, but do not necessarily have expertise in the areas covered. Potential authors should check SJCHC's website for a link to a simplified style sheet guide for article preparation—www.stockton.edu/sjchc/—or just follow the style in this issue. Journal editors will be happy to guide any would-be authors. In certain instances, Stockton editing interns may be assigned to help research topics and/or assist authors with writing.

SAMPLE TOPICS MIGHT INCLUDE:

Biographical sketches of important but forgotten local people; the development or succession of a community's roads, bridges or buildings; local transportation (focused by mode, area or era) and what changes it wrought in the served communities; history of community businesses and industries (wineries, garment factories, agriculture, boat building, clamming, etc.); old school houses, old hotels, or meeting halls; narrative descriptions of local geographical features; essays concerned with folklore, music, arts; and reviews of new local interest publications. Photo essays and old photograph and postcard reproductions are welcome with applicable captions. In short, if a South Jersey topic interests you, it will likely interest *SoJourn*'s readers.

PARAMETERS FOR SUBMISSIONS:
• Submissions must pertain to topics bounded within the eight southernmost counties of New Jersey (Burlington & Ocean Counties and south)
• Manuscripts should be approximately 3,000–4,000 words long (5 to 7 pages of single-spaced text and 9 to 12 pages including images)
• Manuscripts should conform to the *SoJourn* style sheet, available here:
https://blogs.stockton.edu/sjchc/sojourn-style-sheet/
• Manuscripts, if at all possible, should be submitted in digital format (Word- or pdf-formatted documents preferred)
• Images should be submitted as high-resolution tiff- or jpeg-formatted files (editors can assist with digital conversion of photos if necessary). 300 dpi resolution, or higher, preferred
• Complete and appropriate citations printed as endnotes should be employed (see style sheet). If using Word, please use its automated endnote function
• Original submissions only. Copyright licenses for all images must be obtained by the author or should be copyright-free figures and/or figures in the public domain
• If essays are accepted, authors should submit a short 50 to 100 word autobiographical statement
• Articles need to be more than just a chronology of the given topic. The author should be able to properly contextualize the subject by answering such questions as: a) why is this important?; b) what is the impact on the local or regional history? and c) how does it compare to similar events/personages/changes/processes in other localities?

CALL FOR SUBMISSIONS:

Submissions for winter issues are due before September 1; for summer issues, January 15.

Send inquiries or submissions to Thomas.Kinsella@stockton.edu or Paul.Schopp@stockton.edu.

SoJourn

Since 2016, *SoJourn* has supplied over a thousand pages of local history to readers interested in the eight southernmost counties of New Jersey. Please help us spread the word. If you are interested in writing for *SoJourn*, or selling it, contact Thomas.Kinsella@stockton.edu for more information.

Articles Published

SoJourn 1.1 Spring 2016
"Nash's Cabin (Buck Run)" by Richard Watson, 7
"The Future of Transportation: The Bicycle Railway" by Dennis McDonald, 17
"Mary, Mary, Quite Contrary . . ." by Patricia A. Martinelli, 27
"Bipolar State: A Survey and Analysis of South Jersey's Geographical and Cultural Borders" by Robert Lowe Barnett and Steve Chernoski, 33
"Immersion" by Kenneth Tompkins, 49
"Shinplasters: Economic Remnants of New Jersey's Glass Industry" by Todd R. Sciore, 55
"The Burlington Town Plan: From Medieval to Modern" by Robert P. Thompson, 63
"Nature, Naturalists, and South Jersey" by Claude M. Epstein, 75
"Mary Ann and the Cranberry Farm, a Transformative Experience" by Alexis Demitroff, 89

SoJourn 1.2 Winter 2016/17
"Kate Aylesford: Modernity and Place in New Jersey's Pine Barrens" by Matthew G. Hatvany, 7
"Alfred and Muriel: The Story of the J. A. Sweeton House in Cherry Hill, New Jersey" by Brian Stolz as told by Jim Stanton, 19
"School Segregation in the Post-Civil War Era: Burlington County, New Jersey, 1865–1915" by Zachary T. Baer, 25
"Where Blackberries Grew: Margaret Mead in Hammonton" by Patricia Chappine and Mark Demitroff, 37
"A Day on the Bay with Waterman Phil Andersen" by Susan Allen, 45
"South Jersey Fruit Picking Tickets" by Richard Watson, 50
"From Butcher Knife to Scalpel: Four Generations of South Jersey Physicians" by Lisa E. Cox, Edward Hutton and Ruth Hutton-Williams, 63
"Manufacturing from Menhaden: A History in the Mullica Valley" by Kenneth W. Able, 75

"Carabajal, The Jew: A Legend of Monterey, Mexico" by Charles K. Landis, 83
"Reimagining a Remnant of the Past at Stockton" by James Pullaro and Paul W. Schopp, 100

SoJourn 2.1 Summer 2017
"The First African American Excursion to Atlantic City" by Paul W. Schopp, 7
"Proving a Legend: A Submarine in the Rancocas Creek" by Alice Smith, 15
"Brevet Brigadier General Elias Wright: Surveyor Extraordinaire" by Elizabeth G. Carpenter, 23
"Mapping the Mullica Valley: Natural History Landscapes" by Kenneth W. Able, 33
"Off Course in a Raging Sea: Captain William M. Phillips and the Plight of the Schooner Benjamin E. Valentine" by Paul W. Schopp with Anthony Ficcaglia, 45
"Haul Away, Boys!" 53
"Jerseyisms" by Francis E. Lee, 59
"The Rebirth of Buzby's Chatsworth General Store" by R. Marilyn Schmidt, 68
"The Publications of R. Marilyn Schmidt," 78
"The Endicott-Reardon Family Museum" by Rebecca Muller, 81
"Anecdotes and Memoirs of William Boen," 85
"The Coia Map Project" by James Pullaro and Paul W. Schopp, 94

SoJourn 2.2 Winter 2017/18
"Made in Nesco: The Inter-Generational Project of Place-Making" by Mary Jo Kietzman, 7
"Le Balloonist" by Hal Taylor, 23
"Elizabeth C. White's Garden" by Albertine Senske, 28
"Pocahontas on the Delaware: The Intersection of History and Legend in the Historiography of New Jersey" by John W. Lawrence, 39
"Calico or Dobbin's Bog" by Rich Watson, 53
"Plagues and Public Policy: How South Jersey Cleaned Up Its Act" by Claude Epstein, 69
"Stockton University Welcomes Heather Perez: Special Collections Librarian and Archivist" by Amy Krieger, 83
"Ghost Forests in the Mullica Valley: Indicators of Sea-Level Rise" by Kenneth W. Able, Jennifer Walker, and Benjamin P. Horton, 87
"A February Freshet & Breach in the Bank" by Dallas Lore Sharp, 97

SoJourn 3.1 Summer 2018

A thematic issue, discussing the impact of the Revolutionary War on South Jersey. 50% larger than a standard issue.

"Battle of Turtle Gut Inlet" by Zachary T. Baer and Paul W. Schopp, 7

"The Battle of Iron Works Hill" by Salvatore D. Gabriele, 17

"Knight at Egg Harbor" by J. Anthony Harness, 31

"Forgotten Victories" by Jeffery M. Dorwart, 41

"Research into the Battle of Gloucester" by Garry Wheeler Stone, Paul W. Schopp, and Jason R. Wickertsty, 55

"The Battle of the Kegs" by Francis Hopkinson, 74

"Should New Jersey Be Considered the Crossroads of the American Revolution?" by Zachary T. Baer, 77

"When Mad Anthony Came to South Jersey" by Claude M. Epstein, 81

"The Lord's Orders" by J. Anthony Harness, 95

"Born a Peacemaker, Became a Patriot: 1st Lieutenant Jeremiah Leeds" by Norman Reeves Goos, 107

"Notice is Hereby Given: Extracts from Colonial Newspapers," 120

"South Jersey's Revolutionary Battles, Skirmishes, and Future Research," 127

"Cedar Bridge Tavern," 137

"The Atlantic County Veterans Museum," by Jackson Glassey, 141

SoJourn 3.2 Winter 2018/19

"The Southern Pine Barrens: An Ethnic Archipelago" by Elizabeth Marsh, Mark Demitroff, and Paul W. Schopp, 7

"Unexpected Wildlife Refuge: Haven for South Jersey Wildlife" by Nedim C. Buyukmihci, 26

"The Sphinx Woman" by Patricia A. Martinelli, 33

"Horseshoe Crabs: Ancient Migrators" by Kenneth W. Able, Thomas M. Grothues, and Paola López-Duarte, 39

"All Aboard for Amatol, New Jersey" by Daniel J. Dinnebeil, 45

"Unlikely Farmers: Tokens of the Allivine Canning Company" by Todd R. Sciore, 55

"The Newton Union Burial Ground: The Site of Camden County's Origin and The Resting Place of Its Earliest Pioneers" by Robert Shinn, Andrew Levecchia, and Sandra White Grear, 63

"A Century Later: The Spanish Flu in New Jersey" by Brendan Honick, 85

"The Youthful Emigrant: A True Story of the Early Settlement of New Jersey" by Lydia Maria Child, 87

"The Compendium of New Jersey's Crossroads in Folk Music" by Jackson Glassey, 95

"The Bayshore Center: A Unique Maritime Experience on the Delaware Bay" by Jessica English, 99

SoJourn 4.1 Summer 2019

"The Great Island Lying Before Shackamaxon: Petty Island, Lenape-Colonist Relations, and Provincial Rivalries, 1678–1701" by Robert A. Shinn and Jean R. Soderlund, 7

"Captain Wilson & the Walt Whitman Bridge," by Samantha Wyld and Tom Kinsella, 25

"Gary Giberson Talks about Cedar" by Gary Giberson, 30

"Railroads and Forest Fires" by Horace A. Somes Jr. and Paul W. Schopp, 45

"Map of the Skirmish or Battle of Iron Works Hill" by Adam E. Zielinski, 55

"Journal of Thomas Hopkins of the Friendship Salt Works, New Jersey, 1780," 59

"The New Old Cedar Bridge Tavern" by Jessica Chamberlain, 71

"A Window to the Past: Waretown's Glass Negative Postcard Set" by Adele R. Shaw, 74

"Who Was Alick Merriman? A South Jersey Real Photo Postcard Photographer" by Paul W. Schopp, 95

"Shirley Burd Whealton, In Memoriam" by Peter H. Stemmmer, 99

SoJourn **4.2 Winter 2019/20** was unavoidably delayed by Covid, then passed over altogether. Sorry.

SoJourn 5.1 Summer 2020

"History and Ecology of Salt Marsh Ditches in the Mullica Valley" by Kenneth W. Able, 7

"The Kennedy Farm" by Raymond Dudo, 18

"A Bay-Side Outing" by Charles C. Abbott, 29

"Recherché Days on the Rancocas: the Bon-Air Club" by Zachary T. Baer and Paul W. Schopp, 33

"Forgotten Flier of the Pines: The Last Flight of Major William F. Dimas" by John Gregg, 47

"The McNeal Mansion" by Richard Lewis, 53

"History of the McNeal Mansion" by Paul W. Schopp, 57

"Maurice River Memories: Introduction, Summertime 1937, and Tidewater," by Joseph S. Reeves, 65

"Aspirational News: The Woman's Edition of the *Daily Pioneer* and the Presbyterian Improvement

Society in Bridgeton, New Jersey, 1898" by Brittney Ingersoll, 77

"Field Diary of Vernon Bailey: Amatol, New Jersey, May 21, 1919" by Vernon O. Bailey, 87

"Afterword to *The Kidnapped and The Ransomed*: The Still Brothers Trilogy is Complete" by Paul W. Schopp, 91

SoJourn 5.2 Winter 2020/21

"Augustine Herrman and the Mapping of Southern New Jersey" by John W. Lawrence, 7

"Trials and Hardships of Immigrants" by Louis Mounier, 17

"Sea Breeze, New Jersey: A Landscape History" by Samuel Avery-Quinn, 21

"Maurice River Fire Deals Serious Damage to Oyster Houses," images from the Mickey Smith Collection; text by Louis Burgess, 37

"The Forgotten South Jersey Author: Stories of the Pine Barrens" by F. James Bergmann, 43

"The Unnatural History of South Jersey Lagoons" by Kenneth W. Able, 49

"Warbirds Over the Pinelands" by Horace Somes Jr., 55

"Selections from the Noyes Decoy Collection" by Gary Giberson, 67

"Maurice River Memories: Driftwood and Start of the Season" by Joseph S. Reeves, 88

"South Jersey Horse Rescue" by Amanda Clark and Sarahjane Hehre, 98

SoJourn 6.1 Summer 2021

"Careers in Camerawork: Six Photographers of Camden, New Jersey, 1860–1910" by Gary D. Saretzky, 7

" 'Big Saturday' in the Pines: *The Burlington Gazette*, Friday, August 1, 1845" by Edmund Morris, 27

"The Skinny on the Privy: Investigation of the Shipman Mansion Privy" by John W. Lawrence, 33

"The Artist and the Lighthouse" by Hal Taylor, 47

"Jarrad, Last of the Pineys" by George Agnew Chamberlain, 51

"George E. Weber: Burlington County's Greatest Athlete" by Dennis McDonald, 61

"South Jersey Scout Hero" by Erik L. Burro, 69

"Maurice River Memories: 'Quackam's Beach' and 'Relatives' " by Joseph S. Reeves Jr., 75

"In Memoriam Mark Maxwell" by Dennis Niceler & Friends, 81

"The Sum of its Parts: The Making of Port Republic" by Paul W. Schopp, 83

Smith's Meeting House cemetery, Port Republic, January 22, 2022.

www.ingramcontent.com/pod-product-compliance
Lightning Source LLC
Chambersburg PA
CBHW050258090426
42734CB00026B/3498